ROOTS OF THE RIGHT

READINGS IN FASCIST, RACIST AND ELITIST IDEOLOGY

General Editor: GEORGE STEINER
Fellow of Churchill College, Cambridge

RACE AND RACE HISTORY

AND OTHER ESSAYS
BY ALFRED ROSENBERG

RACE AND RACE HISTORY

AND OTHER ESSAYS
BY ALFRED ROSENBERG

Edited and Introduced by
PROFESSOR ROBERT POIS

Associate Professor of History
at Colorado University

1817

HARPER & ROW, PUBLISHERS
New York, Evanston, San Francisco, London

FIRST U.S. EDITION

STANDARD BOOK NUMBER: 06-013364-3

LIBRARY OF CONGRESS CATALOG CARD NUMBER: 73-156571

GENERAL EDITOR'S PREFACE

Reliable estimates put at about seventy million the figure of those dead through war, revolution and famine in Europe and Russia between 1914 and 1945. To all but a few visionaries and pessimistic thinkers of the nineteenth century the image of such an apocalypse, of a return to barbarism, torture and mass extermination in the heartlands of civilized life, would have seemed a macabre phantasy. Much of the crisis of identity and society that has overshadowed twentieth-century history comes from an impulse towards totalitarian politics. The theory of man as a rational animal, entitled to a wide exercise of political and economic decision, of man as a being equally endowed whatever his race, has been attacked at its religious, moral and philosophic roots. The most 'radical' attack— 'radical' in that it demands a total revaluation of man's place in society and of the status of different races in the general scheme of power and human dignity—has come from the Right.

Using the concept of the Fall of Man, of man as an instinctual savage requiring total leadership and repeated blood-letting, a number of elitist, racist and totalitarian dreamers and publicists have offered an alternative statement of the human condition. Fascism, Nazism, the programme of the Falange or the *Croix de Feu*, represent different variants of a related vision. Although this vision is often lunatic and nakedly barbaric, it can provide acute, tragic insights into the myths and taboos that underlie democracy.

Because the political and philosophical programme of the Right has come so near to destroying our civilization and is so alive still, it must be studied. Hence this series of source-readings in elitist, racist and fascist theory as it was articulated in France, Germany, Italy, Spain and other national communities between the 1860s and the Second

GENERAL EDITOR'S PREFACE

World War. These 'black books' fill an almost complete gap in the source material available to any serious student of modern history, psychology, politics and sociology (most of the texts have never been available in English and several have all but disappeared in their original language). But these books also touch on the intractable puzzle of the co-existence in the same mind of profound inhumanity and obvious philosophic and literary importance.

GEORGE STEINER

CONTENTS

A WORD ON ORGANIZATION

The work is divided into five chapters. There are no further subdivisions within the chapters; the various selections within the chapters are linked together with editorial commentary which is printed in italics. Those of Rosenberg's footnotes that are included are indicated in the text with asterisks; the editor's footnotes are numbered.

This volume consists of extracts from the following works by Rosenberg: *Der Mythus des 20. Jahrhunderts; Blut und Ehre, ein Kampf für deutsche Wiedergeburt, Reden und Aufsätze von 1919-1933; Gestaltung der Idee, Blut und Ehre 11. Band;* and *Die Spur des Juden im Wandel der Zeiten.* Full details are given in the Bibliography.

INTRODUCTION

Alfred Rosenberg was born in 1893 of lower-middle-class parents in the Baltic town of Reval. After attending a technical high school in Riga, he received training in architecture in Moscow, but fled Russia during the revolution. He joined the National Socialist German Workers' Party—later the Nazi Party—in 1920, and in 1921 succeeded Dietrich Eckhart as Editor of the *Völkischer Beobachter*. Rosenberg also became Editor of the *Nationalsozialistische Monatshefte* in 1930. In his *Hitler, A Study in Tyranny*, Alan Bullock maintains that Rosenberg and the Bohemian racist, Eckhart, had the greatest influence in moulding Hitler's previously inchoate race-hatred into a quasi-coherent ideology. When Hitler went to prison in 1924, he put Rosenberg at the head of the Nazi Party. In 1929, Rosenberg organized and headed the Kampfbund für deutsche Kultur (Combat League for German Culture). This Munich-based organization was responsible for formulating and enforcing Nazi concepts on aesthetics and the literary arts, concepts which were in part written into law after 1934. In 1930, Rosenberg published his massive work, *Der Mythus des 20. Jahrhunderts*, perhaps the most systematic exposition of racism since Houston Stewart Chamberlain's *Die Grundlagen des XIX Jahrhunderts* (1899), a work to which Rosenberg himself admits being indebted.

Once the Nazis came to power in 1933, Rosenberg was placed at the head of the Aussenpolitisches Amt (Foreign Policy Office), an organization specifically designed to

circumvent normal diplomatic channels in carrying out
sub rosa intrigue. At first, Rosenberg's views on aesthetics
did not go unchallenged even in the party itself, and
between 1933 and the early part of 1934 he engaged in
acrimonious debates with Propaganda Minister Goebbels
and the Nationalsozialistischer Deutscher Studentenbund
(National Socialist Student Alliance) over the future of
German art. Goebbels viewed Rosenberg's *Volkish*
phantasies with some cynicism, while the students pressed
hard for the inclusion of Expressionism in the great
Nazi revolution of spirit. After the blood-purge of June
30th, 1934, the issue was settled by Hitler, who deprecated
'degenerate art'. He did not lend full support to Rosenberg
either, and from that time on Nazi art policy was more
dependent on Hitler's own Biedermeyer-Romantic idio-
syncracies than on the fulfilment of a consistent ideological
programme. (Hitler himself tended less towards *Volkish*
revolution in the arts than towards a revival of pseudo-
Greek architectural forms of the variety so despised by
Rosenberg, and towards a militaristically-tinctured realism.) However, Rosenberg had gained a new office as a
result of the dispute. On January 24th, 1934, he had been
placed at the head of the Amt für die Überwachung der
gesamten geistigen und weltanschaulichen Schulung und
Erziehung der N.S.D.A.P. (Office for Supervision of the
Total Intellectual and Ideological Schooling and Educa-
tion of the National Socialist German Workers' Party).
In spite of this new office, Rosenberg's influence in the
party declined. In 1939, for example, his opposition to a
German-Soviet alliance was ignored, and the Molotov-
Ribbentrop pact followed in August. However, when
Germany unilaterally broke the pact on June 22nd, 1941,
Rosenberg's fortunes rose somewhat.

On July 17th, 1941, Rosenberg was made Reich
Minister for the Eastern Occupied Territories, partly
because of his Eastern background. In this capacity he
was placed in nominal charge of civil administration for
all German-held territories in Eastern Europe. While
Rosenberg occasionally protested against the crimes of
the SS in the Ukraine, indicating correctly that a possible
basis of support was being cut away, he was naturally
silent about the extermination of the Jews. Moreover, all
orders for deportation and confiscation of property
necessarily originated from, or at least passed through,
his office. After Germany's defeat, Rosenberg was brought
to trial at Nuremberg. He was accused and convicted on
the following counts: 1. Conspiracy to commit crimes alleged in other counts; 2. Crimes against peace; 3. War
crimes; 4. Crimes against humanity. He was hanged on
October 16th, 1946.

These were the salient points in the life of Alfred
Rosenberg, chief ideologist for the Nazi Party, a life
which both encompassed and helped to shape a period of
time unparalleled in the history of Western civilization.
This was a period in which one side of German Idealism
expressed itself in rumbling tank columns, mass hysteria
and factories processing human beings. The selected
writings that are presented in this volume represent some
of the most sophisticated rationalizations of modern
times for mass murder and destruction. To the extent that
he was read and believed, and to the extent that he
exercised an ideological influence upon Adolf Hitler,
Alfred Rosenberg was responsible for the bitter flavour of
the twelve-year history of the thousand-year Reich. Yet
one must put the man himself in some perspective.

In intellectual history, Alfred Rosenberg was not much

of an innovator. He was a synthesizer, a man of above-average intelligence who was able to piece together bits and scraps from the darker side of European social and intellectual life. Basically, Rosenberg's ideas on race, the Jews, Christianity and the several international conspiracies, i.e. Jewish, Communist and Masonic, that plagued him can be traced back to four sources:

1. Basic elements of popular Christian anti-Semitism, particularly, as we shall see, that virulent variety of it that emerged from Eastern Europe.

2. Perversions, or unfortunately in some cases simple reiterations of certain teachings which were legacies of the German tradition of political Romanticism. Linked to this would be the general Romantic and/or religious reaction to the French Revolution and the Industrial Revolution.

3. The earlier racist doctrines of Gobineau and Houston Stewart Chamberlain.

4. The distortion of the Nietzschean superman ideal.

First of all, we must see that Rosenberg's attitudes towards the Jews were, in part, simply a recrudescence of centuries-old myths; myths that were in great measure ensconced within the Christian tradition. Rosenberg's attacks upon Jewish 'legalism', particularly his claim that any people which needs a complex law code and commentary lacks a natural morality of its own, can be traced back to certain statements of the early Christian philosopher Justin Martyr (A.D. *c.* 100–*c.* 165), while the medieval tendency to identify the Jew (as well as the Turk and occasionally the pope himself) as the Antichrist has been well documented by Norman Cohn in *The Pursuit of the Millennium* (London, 1957) and by Joshua Trachtenberg in *The Devil and the Jews* (New Haven, 1945). Here, of course, the Jew is depicted as the apostate

crucifier of Christ, and when put in this light he can well
be expected to defile the consecrated host, to make his
matzos from the blood of murdered Christian children
and to drain the blood of Christendom through usury and
fraud. Moreover, as the medieval Church found it
necessary, due to forces of economic necessity, to find a
'place' for the Jews within the established societal framework, chiliastic speculation, such as that arising around
the time of the First Crusade, saw the overthrow of the
established order and overthrow of the Jews as being
coterminous. These forms of popular anti-Semitism were
European, of course, and not peculiar to Germany.
Like the legendary Wandering Jew himself, these doctrines traversed the length and breadth of the Continent.

In the first decade of the twentieth century, however,
popular anti-Semitism achieved its zenith in Eastern
Europe, where the minions of political reaction found it
necessary to deflect public anger over poverty, corruption
and military disaster away from themselves and on to the
most alienated element of the population. Official anti-
Semitism provided a rallying point for the inchoate
demonologies of the oppressed, and the slogan 'Beat the
Yids and save Russia' became the unofficial anthem of
obscurantism and reaction. After the Bolshevik Revolution, when defeat rubbed salt in the wound, disappointed
émigrés saw the Jew—as Richard Wagner had put it—as
the 'plastic demon' of revolution.

In this regard, two factors were of immense significance
for both Alfred Rosenberg and the ideology of the later
Nazi Party: 1. Rosenberg was in Russia during 1917–18
and fled the country during the latter year; and 2. the city
to which he fled, Munich, had become a centre for
White Russian émigrés, all of whom were bitterly anti-

Bolshevik, and a substantial number of whom were equally bitterly anti-Semitic. In *Russia and Germany*, Walter Laqueur documents the influences that extreme right-wing Russian circles exercised upon Rosenberg. Rosenberg had been an anti-Semite since 1917. However, it was from these émigrés (who of course circulated earlier anti-Semitic documents as well as their own) that he seems to have gained a genuine and deep-seated *fear* of the 'International Jew' and the pernicious conspiracy that arose from his alleged lust for power. The White Russian phantasy which claimed that the Bolshevik Revolution was financed by Kuhn, Loeb and Co. in New York, and that it was physically carried out by and for Jews, was readily assimilated by Rosenberg, who included it in his *Pest in Russland*, and in other writings. An ancient myth which posited that the Alliance Israélite Universelle functioned as the leading component of an international Jewish conspiracy found a place not only in Rosenberg's writings of 1919, which are mentioned by Laqueur, but in his 1920 work *Die Spur des Juden im Wandel der Zeiten*. Finally, Laqueur points out that much of what Rosenberg has to say about the Jews can be traced, chapter and verse, to the 1919 'Berlin Letters' of Fyodor Viktorovich Vinberg, a former colonel in the Tsarist armies. In these letters, Vinberg emphasized the aristocratic, inbred nature of the Jews, their control over the world's gold and the press and the pernicious alliance of Judaism and Freemasonry. All of these elements play major roles in Rosenberg's 'analysis' of Jewish history. Vinberg's solution to the Jewish problem — extermination — was never put down *on paper* by Rosenberg or, for that matter, by Hitler, at least before the war. However, the upright soldier of the Tsar was merely being logically consistent. After 1941, the Nazis would do the same. The influence of émigré circles upon Rosenberg was this: they provided him with a popular, conspiratorial view of Jewish history, as well as with a necessary link to centuries-old anti-Semitic traditions. During the medieval period, the Antichrist had been given Jewish form, due to the popular notion that the Jews had killed Christ. However, in modern times, the archetype assumed a different form: the modern-day Jewish world conspirator. As we shall see, the German anti-Semitic tradition was far more sophisticated than that which emerged from the backwaters of Eastern Europe. It was the 'intellectual' (*geistig*) anti-Semitism of a Fichte or a Wagner; or it emerged from the circles of over-precious Romantics, in full flight from the agonies and responsibilities of the industrial age. Eastern-European popular anti-Semitism had a long pedigree, from the seventeenth-century massacres of Bogdan Khmelnitskii to the Black Hundreds. With considerable alacrity, Rosenberg drew upon this legacy.

Mention has been made of the role of German Romantic thinking. By drawing upon this strain Rosenberg was able to justify intellectually both his anti-Semitism and his view of the German people as representing an organic and indivisible *Volk*. Mosse, Viereck, Stern and many others have pointed out that to a not inconsiderable degree twentieth-century racist doctrines can be traced back to the birth of German political Romanticism.[1] This is not the time or place to discuss the movement in detail. It goes without saying,

[1] Kohn, Hans, *The Mind of Germany* (New York, 1960).
Mosse, George L., *The Crisis of German Ideology* (London, 1966; New York, 1964).
Stern, Fritz, *The Politics of Cultural Despair* (Berkeley, 1961).
Viereck, Peter, *Metapolitics: The Roots of the Nazi Mind* (New York, 1961).

however, that Romanticism and, more particularly, the Romantic view of states and peoples, had a profound impact upon German political speculation. Man, in the view of the eighteenth-century political thinkers, was universal. All men were subject to the same forces and permutations of natural law; all men were endowed with the potential to lead a reasonable life in conformity with established principles of this natural law. True, governments might vary from place to place. Voltaire could well be a republican in Geneva and an absolutist in France. Nevertheless, the efficacy of a particular variety of government was directly proportional to the degree to which the government provided the framework and conditions necessary for a people to fulfil their basic human potential. Men could create states and constitutions on the basis of reason, while an impotent or disinterested God watched from the sidelines.

Romanticism, particularly after 1789, was a European rather than a strictly German phenomenon. With its glorification of the mysterious and the abstruse and its elevation of intuition, emotion and nationalism, it represented both a *reaction* against the admittedly brittle doctrines of eighteenth-century rationalism and the French Revolution, and a definite, positive, new worldview. As such, this new approach included Sir Walter Scott in England and Chateaubriand in France. However, we cannot contradict the fact that in Germany Romanticism became politicized to a degree unequalled in the rest of Europe. Johann Gottfried Herder (1744–1803) emphasized the unique nature of a *Volk* to the same degree as the literary Romantics emphasized the unique nature of the artist. Each *Volk* had its own peculiar spirit (*Volksgeist*), which was reflected in its language and in the use of that language in poetry and myth. Herder, who at one point compared humanity to a flower-garden, did not claim that one folk-spirit was superior to another. However, by claiming that humanity was *not* one, but a conglomeration of various national individualities, Herder seemed to be saying that a man fulfilled his own humanity only through the nation, the larger individuality to which he was bound by shared historical experience and language. Johann Gottlieb Fichte (1762–1814), originally a philosopher of the Kantian school, became a German nationalist after the Prussian defeat at Jena (1806). In this context, he used crude approximations of the Herder approach to claim German *supremacy* over all other peoples. Fichte claimed that the unchanging nature of the German language testified to a strength of character and will unknown to other peoples. The very profundity of German philosophy spoke of a folk-spirit which was both more serious and more honestly involved in the world than that, say, of the French. Fichte combined these nationalistic views with a strong dislike of the established nobility and the Jews. What Fichte seemed to be establishing philosophically and historically, the poets Arndt and Körner and the somewhat cruder patriot, Father Jahn, established on a less intellectual level: the heroic, self-sacrificing individuality of *Volk*. In response to political fragmentation and national humiliation, Germany's intellectual community —or at least that portion of it that rallied to Prussia as a centre both of resistance to Napoleon and possible national unification—utilized the Romantic values of intuition, folk-spirit and autonomy as normative categories of national political life. As the nineteenth century moved on, individuality became transformed into *race*.

Rosenberg's debt to such thinking is obvious. The peculiar, soil-and-history-bound nature of a given *Volk* was a necessary underpinning of National Socialist ideology (as we will see, Rosenberg paid homage to Herder in his *Der Mythus des 20. Jahrhunderts*). If pure and separate race was to be the new ideal of human existence, universal man had to be eliminated. Furthermore, the pronounced anti-Semitism of Fichte and such latter-day Romantics as Wagner, de Lagarde and Langbehn provided Rosenberg with both rationalization and intellectual precedent. German metaphysical debasement of the Jew complemented that religious and social debasement that had been his lot throughout Europe since medieval times. Rosenberg's ideas on religion—his attacks upon Pauline Christianity and upon the Jewish and 'un-Nordic' conception of creation, his glorification of St John as representing an 'aristocratic' variety of 'positive Christianity', his call for an essentially 'national' religion—all these curious elements can be found in the writings of Fichte, while emphasis upon a de-Judified 'national' church was also a characteristic of Paul de Lagarde (né Bötticher, 1827–91).

Rosenberg was definitely indebted to the well-established tradition of German Romanticism, particularly to its political strain. From it he derived concepts of national individuality, collective national consciousness, anti-Semitism, racial supremacy and a general anti-urban bias (one that of course reinforced anti-Semitism, because Jews were traditionally associated with cities). It was a tragedy of German history that Rosenberg could well consider himself to be a *Kulturmensch* while being a racist. In German intellectual history, the two terms were not mutually exclusive.

An important aspect of the post-1789 period was the reaction against the French Revolution and the Napoleonic conquests which followed it. We have already considered this with regard to political Romanticism. There was, however, another aspect to this reaction, one which was readily assimilated by Rosenberg. This was the tendency of many conservatives to view the French Revolution as stemming from some sort of conspiracy, particularly one in which the Illuminati and Freemasons were involved. The writings of the Abbé Barruel were of great importance here, and Rosenberg drew considerable spiritual sustenance from them. Conspiracy theories were rife after the French Revolution, and although these usually involved Freemasonry rather than Judaism, the fact that numerous Jews did belong to this secret society allowed many — Rosenberg included — to view it as an arm of the international Jewish conspiracy. Not only Germany, but Europe as a whole had a well-established habit of explaining away revolution and national disaster as being due to the secretive activities of treacherous personalities or organizations. This, too, served Rosenberg well.

The third substantial influence on Rosenberg is to be found in the writings of two 'scientific' racists, Arthur de Gobineau (1816–82) and Houston Stewart Chamberlain (1855–1927). Arthur de Gobineau, a French diplomat — whose selected political writings (*Gobineau,* edited by Professor Michael D. Biddiss), are available in the Roots of the Right Series (Harper & Row, New York, 1970) — was the first to view human history in essentially racial terms. In his major work, *Essai sur l'inégalité des races humaines* (Paris, 1853), Gobineau stated that human history was race history. For a given civilization to survive, purity of the race which created it had to be maintained. If racial lines were polluted by the introduction of inferior blood, racial 'bastardization' would set in, and the civilization would fall. However, the 'Aryan' race could not intermix with any other, because all other races were inferior and any mixture would lead to bastardization and racial extinction. Miscegenation was, unfortunately, unavoidable and therefore Gobineau's outlook with regard to the future of civilization was bleak. As Mosse points out in *The Crisis of German Ideology*, Gobineau's ideas reached Germany in 1894, when Ludwig Schemann founded a Gobineau Society. Schemann was also a member of the Richard Wagner Circle and the Pan-German League, and was able to disseminate Gobineau's ideas through these two rather prestigious groups. Rosenberg made much use of such terms as 'Aryan', 'race-purity', 'racial bastardization', etc. He was indebted to Gobineau for them.

Houston Stewart Chamberlain, to whom Rosenberg approvingly refers on several occasions, was the son of an English admiral. Because of his obsessive love of things German, he became a German citizen, eventually marrying the daughter of Richard Wagner. After this auspicious beginning, Chamberlain devoted a substantial portion of his remaining days to glorifying the German race. The idea of a *Mythus*, a mysterious super-rational infusion of spirit which binds a given people to eternal forces of nature, a concept which was central to Rosenberg's philosophy, really originated in the writings of Chamberlain, who published his most significant work, *Die Grundlagen des XIX Jahrhunderts*, in 1899. In this tome Chamberlain glorified the German as embodying an inward purity unrivalled by any other nation. The German was characterized by a mysterious soul of an almost sacred nature, and it was this mysterious yet concrete soul—Chamberlain referred to it as the German 'religion'—which set the German apart from his archetypal 'race-foe', the Jew. Furthermore, Chamberlain drew a distinction between so-called 'scientific' spirit and the 'religious' spirit, mentioned above. Both were important, and both were prominent aspects of the overall German 'spirit'. However, it was this inviolable religious spirit which shaped the German *Kultur* and differentiated it from mere *civilization*. Like Gobineau, Chamberlain made use of a number of terms which are found in the writings of Rosenberg. As we will see, Rosenberg gives Chamberlain credit for coming up with that most meaningful of terms, 'race-chaos'.

Gobineau and Chamberlain were 'scientific' racists. While certain mystical elements were involved in their writings, particularly those of Chamberlain, they claimed to have discovered substantive laws which underlie the growth and death of nations. Of particular importance here was Chamberlain's claim that psychic conditions were reflected in the *physical* form of a given individual. This allowed one to judge a man's blood and spirit by using a given physical criterion. The influence of so-called 'scientific' racism was great in German anthropology and Rosenberg was thus able to surround his speculations with an aura of science.

The final substantive influence on Rosenberg was exercised by that most tragic of individualists, Friedrich Nietzsche. Perhaps Rosenberg knew that Nietzsche was not a German nationalist and that, in fact, he despised German nationalism. Perhaps he knew that Nietzsche glorified the Old Testament, particularly its prophetic tradition, and found it to be superior to the tradition of

the New Testament. He might also have known that
Nietzsche's sister, widow of the noted racist Bernhard
Förster, had carried out a rather questionable editing job
on Nietzsche's writings. If he knew this, we can well say
that Rosenberg deliberately distorted Nietzsche in order
to make him appear as a prototype *Blut-und-Boden* racist
and a German nationalist. However, we would have to
admit that Nietzsche himself made it relatively easy for
any reasonably literate individual to do the same. First
of all, Nietzsche was hardly a systematic philosopher.
In spite of the obvious coherence of such works as
Götzendämmerung (1889) Nietzsche, particularly in his last
days of sanity, spoke in aphorisms and often in disjointed
and seemingly illogical phrases. His occasionally inchoate
ramblings about 'will to power', the 'superman' and
'values of the herd' — terms which were once part of his
more systematic critiques — made it easy for one to view
him as an heroic, blood-conscious man of the sword.
As many of his critics have pointed out, Nietzsche's
'superman' probably would have spoken Greek; his
obvious preference for Dionysian rather than Apollonian
elements of Greek life proved to be an embarrassment to
Rosenberg who, in keeping with his racial theories, had
to attribute these Dionysian strains to inferior, Asiatic
races. There can be little doubt that Rosenberg distorted
Nietzsche; whether he did this consciously or not will
probably remain unknown, and as we have said Nietzsche
rendered such distortion all too easy. By the 1920s he had
become an important deity in the pantheon of Germany's
radical right. Rosenberg used the aesthetic Nietzschean
'superman' as a generic term to mean of the purest
Nordic lineage. Nietzsche's pronounced anti-Christianity,
his contempt for the Socratic tradition and his glorification

of the caste-system of ancient India were elements which
fit in well with Rosenberg's speculations. All that he had
to do was to remould them in the form of race categories,
then the SS man could push the aesthete aside and crown
his own blond brow with the laurels of the superman.
When Rosenberg summoned Germans to defend the
threatened *Vaterland*, he did so in the name of Friedrich
Nietzsche.

Rosenberg's distorted treatment of Nietzsche brings
up the question of distortion in his works as a whole.
There can be little doubt that at times Rosenberg consciously distorted ideas and events, while at other times—
with the Talmud, for instance—he simply did not know
what he was talking about. Yet, as in the case of Nietzsche,
Rosenberg seldom lied outright. The weapon he used—
and to great effect—was that of the half-truth. For
example, Rosenberg claims that the Talmud condemned
agricultural pursuits in favour of those of business, and
quotes the opinion of Rabbi Eleazer, recorded in Yebamoth 63a. However, in claiming that this indicated a
Talmudic preference for business, Rosenberg showed how
little he knew about the Talmud. The *Gemara*—the
second portion of the Talmud—which Rosenberg uses
to attack the 'materialism and cunning' of Judaism, is
really a record of discussion and disputation. For any one
opinion, an opposing one can usually be found. This may
be readily appreciated when we note that in the same
section, Yebamoth 63a, in which Rabbi Eleazer deprecates farming, men are exhorted to *become* men through
owning and tilling land. Furthermore, examination of
the Talmudic writings (e.g. Kiddushin 30b and 82a)
would show that the most esteemed occupation was
neither farming nor business, but handicrafts. It cannot

be denied that various writers indicated that there was a qualitative difference between Jews and non-Jews. However, Rosenberg's assertion that Jewish law *as a whole* did not view non-Jews as human beings is absolutely false. Maimonides, for example, says that any form of cheating or theft is forbidden, whether directed against Jew or non-Jew, and the Talmud, in various places, exhorts Jews to be loyal to the state (Aboth 3, 2); to help heathen poor and sick; even to assist in burying heathen dead (Gittin 61a) and supporting their aged (Kiddushin 32b); and to deal honestly and fairly with non-Jews 'for sanctification of the name'. When Rosenberg claims to have discovered a secret fount of Jewish deceitfulness in Traktat Pesachim 113a and 113b, where it is written, ' ... Canaan has taught its sons five things; to love one another, to love theft, to love dissolution, to hate thy master and to never speak the truth,' he only indicates his own spiritual confusion. The Canaan referred to here is that of pre-Israelite times. As Jacob Katz has pointed out in his *Exclusiveness and Tolerance* (Oxford, 1961), a great deal of anti-Gentile bitterness can be found in Jewish writings. Sectarian bitterness and recrimination is always especially ferocious and painful. But in Judaism, as in Christianity, the obverse of this can always be found as well.

Although Judaism was his primary target, Rosenberg's universalist interests compelled him to pursue the half-truth into other realms. He is, of course, correct when he states that the last centuries of Rome saw political chaos and the rise of Orientals to prominence in Roman political life and in the army. However, his claim that the papacy is derived from a recrudescence of the Etruscan priesthood, the Haruspices, is ludicrous, as is his broader assumption that Christianity worked assiduously for the fall of Rome. As is well known, one of those who most profoundly appreciated the *necessity* for Rome was St Augustine. Rosenberg is correct, of course, when he attacks the medieval period for belief in witchcraft, an aberration which he then lays at the feet of Christianity. In fact, belief in witches hardly constitutes a substantive portion of Christianity, although the medieval Christian probably believed in them. It would seem rather that belief in witches, lycanthropy and associated super-stitions was important in that *sub rosa* folk-religion which Rosenberg extolled as representing Nordic resistance to Rome. Of course, Rosenberg has a point when he attacks the medieval Church for simony and for misuse of the doctrine of indulgences. What he fails to mention is that the doctrine of indulgences was something which developed quite late in the history of Christianity, not really emerg-ing until the fourteenth and fifteenth centuries, and that when it did emerge its abuses were assailed by a consider-able number of good Catholics. In attacking St Paul as being a Jewish, anti-*Volk* legalist and then upholding Luther as something of a *Volk* hero, Rosenberg is being logically inconsistent in that St Paul was Luther's guiding light. Moreover, despite his vicious anti-Jewish stance, Luther was about as far from being a racist as anyone could be. Needless to say, Rosenberg's presentation of Christianity, and his differentiation between a Nordic 'positive' Christianity and that 'negative' variety emanat-ing from Rome and upheld by the major Christian faiths of modern times, is inaccurate and full of half-truths.

Rosenberg naturally both accepted and expressed some of the general right-wing myths that were abroad in Germany during the inter-war period: the Social Demo-crats were treacherous and unpatriotic; the German

army had been stabbed in the back by a coterie of
Communists, Jews and Democrats; the Jews of the British
Empire had created animosity between two Nordic
peoples, the English and the Germans. Rosenberg was
unable to accept either the reality of military disaster or
Ludendorff's hysterical acquiescence in it in September
1918, which, of course, he never mentioned.

Rosenberg did not confine his distortions to the areas of
religious and contemporary history. Ideological consis-
tency led him to venture into the foggy realm of *Kulturgeschichte*. Here he managed to transform the Egyptians
and ancient Greeks into blond-worshipping Aryans,
Herder into an anti-humanist, Leopold von Ranke into
an adherent of Nordic *Volk*-philosophy, and Goethe into
both a nationalist and an anti-Semite. Was this deliberate
distortion? In some cases yes, in others no. As a theologian
there were certain substantial lacunae in Rosenberg's
Bildung, and there can be little doubt that many of his
statements were made out of ignorance. However, with
regard to such people as Goethe, Herder and others it
would appear that Rosenberg, if not the ideal *gebildeter
Mensch*, still knew enough about these seminal figures to
realize what was distortion and what was not. The most
terrifying aspect of all of this, however, was the basic
idealism that both lay behind and rationalized this
distortion. Half-truths would become truths and the
crooked made straight if they were salved by the healing
balm of the Nordic *Mythus*.

As we will see, Rosenberg was eminently a utopian, so
much so that once the Nazis actually attained power
many of his odder notions—such as his theories on the
Ordnensstaat, plastic arts and the artisan—were self-
consciously forsaken. (A good study of the realities of the

Hitlerian take-over can be found in David Schoenbaum's *Hitler's Social Revolution*.) Nevertheless, the call for a 'revolution of spirit', as opposed to anti-*Volk* class war, a strong anti-urban bias and the revival of an almost medieval sense of honour and chivalry were never expunged from the Nazi programme. In such organizations as the SS, utopianism remained predominant. In 1944 and early 1945, 'idealistic heights' were scaled when trains needed for the movement of troops and supplies were used to transport masses of the racially impure to their deaths. This 'idealism' and the concept of 'revolution of the spirit' were two of the biggest drawing cards of Nazism. 'Idealism', as opposed to the seemingly sterile doctrine of dialectical materialism, endowed the Nazi Party with a kind of super-political and super-class sanctity which, in a nation with weak traditions of political pluralism, was very useful; while a revolution which did not demand class upheaval but merely *Volk*-consciousness was preferable to one which called for the rigours of class warfare.

Rosenberg's conception of the state was also utopian in the extreme. Like most of Germany's Romantics, he eschewed the Hegelian tradition which defined the state as being the objectification of God on earth and hence placed it in the centre of human affairs. Indeed, Rosenberg displayed a predominantly anarchic attitude; the state obtained its validity only through the will of the collective *Volk*, while a *Volk* was defined as being a group of individuals bound together by blood and soul. The unity of *Volk* was inviolable, and theories of class war could have originated only from the un-*Volkish* mind of a Jew, in this case Marx. If the blood and soul were to become translated into community, the atomistic alienation of the individual would end and all labour receive its justification. In this way, of course, the role of the National Socialist movement—as embodying the will of the *Volk*—superseded that of the state, which ideally was to be merely its administrative and juridical appendage.

After 1935, Rosenberg's position in the party declined somewhat, and after the Second World War most of Hitler's surviving minions claimed not to have read Rosenberg or not to have taken him very seriously (G. M. Gilbert's *Nuremberg Diary* is revealing on this). There can be little doubt, though, that Rosenberg's early influence on Hitler was very great and that the racially pure, youth-oriented, bucolic *Volksstaat* remained as an ideal, even if aspects of it had to be sacrificed to mundane matters of diplomacy and economics.

Also, it must be obvious that the writings of Alfred Rosenberg, more than those of any other individual, were designed to constitute—and indeed did constitute—the *complete* Nazi ideology; hence their great influence, even if often at second-hand. An individual Nazi might not have been terribly interested in the racial significance of Etruscan pottery; however, his own particular basic beliefs were both apotheosized and rationalized in the writings of Alfred Rosenberg.

The social and economic historian might well protest that the Nazi Revolution was, if not precisely a bourgeois counter-revolution, then at least a phenomenon of the German middle class, particularly of white-collar interests, farmers, independent artisans, etc. From this he might further extrapolate that such things as ideologies, although admittedly interesting, are mere epiphenomena and therefore of secondary importance. There can be little doubt that the Nazi Revolution was in fact largely bourgeois in origin and support. However, if *what* it represented was common to all the states of the Western world, *how* it represented it was not. The gas chamber, the soap factory, the undeniable 'idealism' of the Hitler Jugend and SS—these cannot be explained on the basis of socio-economic analysis. To be able to enslave millions, murder small children and yet speak of 'decency' and *Kultur*, one needed 'ideals'. Rosenberg is representative of the hideous idealism that underlay the achievements of Heydrich, Kaltenbrunner, Eichmann and Himmler. It was because of this idealism and utopianism that Eichmann, on trial for his life in Jerusalem, could claim that he had always attempted to adhere to the spirit of the Kantian categorical imperative.

As mentioned before one of the most convenient aspects of the Nazi ideology was its implacable belief in conspiracies. Conspiracy theories are always rife when human beings contemplate the annoyances and frustrations of existence: war results from conniving capitalists disposing of surplus production and fighting over new markets; the fall of the ancien régime was due to the perfidious work of Freemasons; communists are trying to weaken America by putting fluoride in its water; birth control is a racist plot to diminish the number of blacks. Naturally, conspiracies do take place and most people believe in them at one time or another. However, the extremists of left and right are united in a unique elevation of conspiracy to being a working side-effect of *Weltanschauung*. It might well be true that conspiratorial explanations of events are the gossamer phantasms of second-rate minds; but few minds in any given field are truly first rate, and even these are often shaken in times of crisis.

Alfred Rosenberg and the party for which he wrote and

fought are dead. But the impedimenta of destructive idealism can be found in many places. Theories of racial supremacy, mutterings about Zionist world conspiracies, calls for action for the sake of action—each of these exists today as a testimony to spiritual poverty in the face of those substantive challenges posed by life; and Rosenberg's alternately snide and vitriolic attacks on non-spiritual empiricism and 'fact-mongering' are approximated by those post-war 'idealists', who employ such terms as 'communism', 'fascism', 'imperialism' and 'Americanism' with an abandon that is both heroic and perverse. 'Spiritual attitude'—to use a favourite term of Rosenberg's —ideology, *Weltanschauung*: these have always been the normative foundation of political activity. We see that today, also, the political leader is successful to the degree that he is able to resolve the dialectical contradiction between belief and reality in favour of the former. Indeed, the poignant succession of myths which in part constitutes human history seems to prove the validity of Rosenberg's claim that *Mythus* is truer and more powerful than all endeavours at rational religion or philosophy.

ROBERT POIS

I. RACE AND RACE HISTORY

The extracts in this chapter are taken from the preface to the 'Race and Mythus' section of the 1938 edition of Rosenberg's Der Mythus des 20. Jahrhunderts.

The power struggles of today are manifestations of an inner collapse. Already, *all* the state systems of 1914 have fallen, even if in part they still have formal existence. Furthermore, social, religious and ideological [*Weltanschauliche*] concepts and values also lie shattered. No commanding principle, no high Idea exercises uncontested dominion over the lives of peoples. Group struggles against group, party against party, national values against internationalistic doctrines, petrified imperialism against encroaching pacifism. Finance entangles states and peoples in its golden fetters, while economics becomes nomadized and life uprooted.

As indicative of world revolution, the World War laid bare the tragic fact that while millions sacrificed their lives these sacrifices accrued to the benefit of forces other than those for which armies were ready to die. The war dead are the victims of a catastrophe-stricken epoch which had long since become valueless; at the same time, however, ... they are the martyrs of a new day, of a new belief.

The blood that had died is beginning to come to life anew. In its mystical patterns a new cellular-structure of the German *Volk*-soul is developing. Present and past are suddenly appearing in a new light, and as a result we have a new mission for the future. The actions of history and the future no longer signify class struggle or warfare between Church dogmas, but rather the conflict between blood and blood, race and race, people and people. And this means combat between spiritual values.

Observation of history from a racial standpoint is a heuristic principle which will soon become self-explanatory. Worthy individuals are serving this principle already. In the not-too-distant future these hosts will be able to fulfil themselves as the founders of a new world-picture.

However, the values of race-soul, which stand behind the new world-picture as driving forces, still have not been brought to living consciousness. *Soul means race viewed from within. And, vice-versa, race is the externalization of soul.* Awakening the race-soul to life means recognizing its highest value and, under the direction of this value, providing organic configuration for the other values—in state, *Kultur* and religion. This is the task of our century: to create a new human type from a new life-*Mythus*. Courage is needed for this task, courage on the part of each individual member of the race; courage on the part of the entire ascending race; indeed, courage on the part of generations yet unborn. For the dispirited will never master chaos, nor will cowards ever build a world. Whoever wants to strive forward must burn his bridges behind him. Whoever sets out on a great journey must leave behind all old household effects. Whoever strives for the highest must humble the inferior. The new man of the approaching first German Reich will have but one answer for all doubts and questions: Alone, I will!

Even if many today have already affirmed *these* words in a deep, inward manner, no organization can be based upon the thoughts and conclusions that have been

laid down in these pages. Throughout, these are *personal*
beliefs, not programme points of the political movement
to which I belong. This movement has its own great,
special mission, and *as an organization* it must hold itself
distant from clashes of a religious or denominational-
political nature just as it must not profess allegiance to a
particular philosophy of art or to a particular style of
architecture. Therefore, it cannot be held responsible for
what has been set down here. Conversely, philosophical,
religious and artistic convictions are truly established only
under conditions of personal freedom of conscience. This
is the case here. However, this work is not directed to
those who, happily and inflexibly, live and function within
their respective fields; but rather to those who have
inwardly torn themselves loose from such beliefs and who
now seek out new ideological affiliations, but have been
unable to attain them. The fact that today these people
number millions obliges each comrade to assist, through
deep reflection, both himself and other seekers.

1. *Race and race-soul*

Today an epoch begins in which world history must be
rewritten. The old images of the human past are faded;
the outlines of the actors seem blurred and their inner
motivation falsely depicted, while the collective essence
(of the human past) has been almost completely mis-
understood. A life-feeling, both young and yet known in
ancient times, is pressing towards articulation; a *Weltanschauung* is being born and, strengthened through will, is
beginning to struggle with older forms, hallowed usages
and accepted substances. This struggle is no longer
merely an historical one, but one of principle. It is not
confined to a few particular areas; but it is a general one.

It is taking place not only in the tree-tops but in the roots.

This is the sign of our time: turning away from limitless Absolutism, i.e. the abandonment of a value which subsumes all that is experiential and organic; a value which, in order to establish either peacefully or by force a superhuman community of *all souls*, posits itself as the singular Ego. At one time, the 'Christianizing of the world' and its redemption through the Second Coming constituted such a final goal. There appeared as another goal the dream of 'humanizing humanity'. Both ideals have been buried in bloody chaos and in the rebirth that occurred in the experiences of the World War. In spite of this, first one and then the other of these goals always manages to find an ever more fanatical priesthood and body of supporters. These are cold phenomena, no longer possessed of life. A belief which dies in the soul can no longer be awakened from the dead.

Humanity, the cosmopolitan Church and the self-mastering Ego torn loose from any variety of blood membership — these are no longer absolute values for us. Rather, they have become dubious, in part, completely brittle statements of a polarity-less rape of nature, nurtured by abstraction. The nineteenth-century flight to Darwinism and Positivism was the first great, if purely bestial, protest against the lifeless and empty ideals of those forces which had once descended upon us from Syria and Asia Minor; forces which had prepared spiritual degradation. An all-intrusive Christianity and humanitarianism despised the streams of blood-red, real life which course through the veins of all true *Volk* art and every culture; our blood was robbed of its spiritual nature through chemical formulae which 'explained' it. Today, however, an entire race is beginning to suspect that values will be created and preserved only where blood-law determines the Idea [*Idee*] and activities of man, be they conscious or unconscious. Man fulfils the command of the blood, in cult and in life, in the realm of the subconscious, 'true to nature' as that happy phrase describes this harmony between nature and civilization. Gradually, however, civilization, in providing conscious-ness and reasons for all subconscious activities, becomes ever more intellectual, and as time goes on establishes not creative tension, but discord. In such a manner reason and understanding divorce themselves from race and nature. Torn loose from the bonds of blood and racial order, the individual being sacrifices his absolute, unrepresentable spiritual form; he tears himself farther and farther away from his natural milieu, mixing enemy blood with his own. And it is this blood crime which causes the death of personality, *Volk*, race and civilization. No one who despises the religion of the blood is immune to its revenge; not the Indian, Persian, Greek or Roman. Nordic Europe also will be unable to escape this revenge if it does not do a *volte-face* and turn away from spiritually empty shib-boleths and bloodless absolute ideas, and begin to draw confidently once again on the buried well-springs of its own unique life-juices and values ...

Racial history is, therefore, both natural history and spiritual mystique. However, on the other hand, the history of the blood religion is a great universal tale of the rise and fall of peoples, their heroes and thinkers, their discoverers and artists.

Today history can probe more deeply into the past than earlier generations could have dared to hope. The monu-ments of all peoples now lie strewn before us. Excavations of the most ancient traces of human art allow us to make a comparison of the driving strengths of cultures. Myths have been collected, from Iceland to Polynesia; most of the treasures of the Mayas recovered. Today, geology has attained such a level as to be able to map out periods which occurred tens of thousands of years before our own time. Under-sea explorations are raising great masses of lava from the depths of the Atlantic Ocean—lava from the peaks of suddenly-submerged mountains, in whose valleys cultures once existed before one or many fearful catastrophes broke over them.

Geographers tell us of a continent between North America and Europe, remnants of which we see in Greenland and Iceland. They also reveal to us that on the far side of the high northern islands (Novaya Zemlya) there exist old waterlines which lie more than one hundred metres over the present ones. This phenomenon points to the probability that the North Pole has shifted position and that there was once a much milder climate in the present Arctic region. All this together puts the ancient sagas about Atlantis in a new light. Apparently it is no longer completely out of the question that where today the waves of the Atlantic roar and mighty icebergs wander, a flourishing continent once towered over the deluge; a continent on which a creative race nurtured a great, far-reaching culture and sent its children out into the world as sea-voyagers and warriors. However, even if this Atlantis hypothesis should be proved untenable, it will be necessary to accept the existence of a Nordic, prehistoric culture-centre.

Long ago we had to abandon the notion of there being a homogeneous origin for the myths, art and religious forms of all peoples. On the contrary, well-established evidence of saga-diffusion from people to people and the correlation of these sagas with different groups of people reveals that most of the basic myths have a definite point of origin; their place(s) of creation. Moreover, in their external forms, they are apparently comprehensible only to a certain group. This proves that great migrations of races and peoples took place during even the earliest times. Thus, the solar (sun) myth is not to be understood as being indicative of a 'general developmental order', but rather as a myth which originated *at that point* where the phenomenon of the sun must have been felt as a cosmic experience; this would be in the far north, where a sharp division of the seasons was significant. Only there could the sun impress into the innermost recesses of the soul that certainty of its role as the life-renewing, creative, world primal force. That old, despised hypothesis which stated that once, from a Northern creative point—which we will call Atlantis, even if we do not literally believe in a sunken continent of Atlantis—swarms of warriors spread out, which might explain the continuously recurring Nordic longing to conquer distant lands: this hypothesis seems probable today. These streams of Atlantians sailed their own swan and dragon ships to the Mediterranean, to Africa, towards Kutscha in Central Asia and probably even to China; they also sailed to the southern portion of the North American continent.

... We find the Nordic boat with swan prow and three sheets in pre-Dynastic Egypt. Furthermore, its oarsmen were the later master race [*Herrenvolk*] of the warrior Amorites, people whom Sayce[1] knew as being fair-skinned and blue-eyed. They pressed towards North Africa as a stalwart hunting clan which gradually

[1] A. H. Sayce was a noted late-19th-century English historian, whose speciality was the ancient Near East. (Ed.)

subjugated the entire area, while a portion of them migrated through Syria towards Babylon. The Berbers, who even today are in large measure fair-skinned and blue-eyed, do not trace their ancestry back to the later Vandal incursions, but rather to the primeval Atlantic-Nordic migrations. Today, for example, a not insignificant number of the hunting Kabylen [*Jäger-Kabylen*] are still of unblemished Nordic ancestry (e.g. the blond Berbers constitute ten per cent of the population of the region around Constantinople; around Djebel Scheschor the number is even greater). The ruling strata of ancient Egypt recognized fine features on the faces of conquered peoples. Presumably these 'Hamites' are an admixture of Atlantians and the original negroid inhabitants. Around 2400 B.C. there appear reliefs of men—those 'blond Libyans' of whom Pausanias later reports—with fair skin, red-blond hair and blue eyes. We find the 'four races' of Egypt depicted upon the monuments of Thebes: Asian, Negro, Libyan and Egyptian. The last were depicted in red. However, the Libyans are shown as having blue eyes, and as being bearded and white-skinned. Pure Nordic types are to be found in the tombs of Senye of the Eighteenth Dynasty. The woman on the pylon of Horemheb at Karnak is a Nordic type, while the swan-boat people appear on the temple-relief to Medinet-Habu the Tsakkarai (Teukroi), founder of 'Phoenician' navigation. Light-skinned men with golden-yellow hair are depicted on the tombs of Medinet-Eurob. At the latest [1927] excavation of the pyramid of Cheops at Mastabas, it was discovered that the 'princes and Queen Meres-Anah' were depicted as having blond hair. In all the sagas, the legendary, myth-enshrouded Queen Nitokris is described as being blonde.

These are all racial monuments to a primeval, Nordic conquest of North Africa. The Amorites founded Jerusalem, and they established a Nordic strain in late Galilee, i.e. in the 'heathen region' from which Jesus was supposed to have come. They were reinforced by the Philistines who had also brought the Nordic type of ship (stem-post symbol of hatchet and three leaves) to Syria, where it had been unknown up to that time.

The location of the primal homeland of the Nordic race will probably remain undetermined. Like the inhabitants of the South Atlantic who streamed towards Africa and Southern Asia, the inhabitants of the North Atlantic bore the sun god of Europe to northern Asia; in fact, all the way to Sumeria, whose year once began with the day of the winter solstice! Recent investigations in Iceland and Scotland point to the possibility of an early Stone-Age migration. Moreover, the ancient Irish ideal of beauty was milk-white skin and blond hair. However, this ideal was changed with the invasion of a dark, round-headed race. While it is still rather doubtful, later investigations must ascertain whether or not the oldest cult-symbols, the first cave-drawings, were in fact the roots of the linear script of pre-Dynastic Egypt. Such investigations might also determine whether other varieties of writing throughout the world trace their ancestry to this 'Atlantic' form of symbol. Whatever comes from this investigation, however, it cannot alter the fact that the 'sense of world history' has spread out from the North over the entire world; a sense that was borne by a blue-eyed, blond race which, in several massive waves, has determined the spiritual physiognomy of the world, while at the same time determining what aspects of it must perish. The following phenomena can be identified with the period of

migrations: the saga-enshrouded march of the Atlantians
through North Africa; the advance of the Aryan to the
Persian-Indian realm, followed by Dorians, Macedonians
and Latins; the progression of the Germanic *Völk-
erwanderung*; the colonizing of the world by the Germanic-
natured Occident ...

*   *   *

*One of the earliest regions to be settled by the heroic Nordic spirit
was the Indian sub-continent. Rosenberg did not spare the super-
latives in describing the Aryans' (i.e. Nordic) role in India,
Persia and Greece.*

The Indian, as a born master, felt his soul expand to be
a breath of life which filled the entire universe. At the
same time he felt the world throb within his bosom.
Even Nature herself, mysterious, rich and all-generous,
could not entice him out of this metaphysical profundity.
A life of action which had been recognized by the old
teachings of the Upanishads as being an indispensable
precondition for even the ascetic thinker, began, before
the wanderer's eyes, to fade into the universe of the soul;
and this course from variegated colour to the white light of
knowledge led to the most grandiose of attempts to
overthrow nature through reason. No doubt, at that time
many exceptional or aristocratic Indians succeeded in
surmounting the mundane world. However, later Indians
were bequeathed only the teachings, not their vital,
living, racial preconditions. Gradually they lost all
understanding of the blood-colour sense of *Varna*.[2]

---

[2] *Varna* is an old Sanskrit word which means colour. It implies the
division of a group of people according to colour, i.e. the means of dis-
tinguishing between the Aryan invaders of India—it was they who coined
the term—and the original Dravidian inhabitants. (Ed.)

Today, the application of Varna to the area of technical division of labour represents the most hideous mockery of one of world history's wisest insights. The later Indian did not know of Blood, Ego and All, but only of the last two entities. The vital attempt to grasp Ego in itself died within him. The Indian fell heir to a race-crime whose offspring can be seen today as the spiritually impoverished bastards who seek to cure their crippled being in the waters of the Ganges ...

The Indian monist, even after he had 'overcome', through rational decision, the spiritual polarity of Ego/All in favour of the latter pole, was also concerned with finally eliminating the reciprocal and mutually-conditioning polar relationship which saw freedom conditioning nature while nature conditioned freedom. He was therefore not inclined to consider race and personality as concepts which possessed a high value. The late-Indian spiritual monist saw nature as something unreal, or as a bad dream. All that is real is embodied in the world-soul (Brahman) and in its eternal rebirth in individualities (Atman). Above all, there resulted from this turning away from nature a continuous weakening of the earlier clear representation and conception of race. Instinct was enticed from its earthly kingdom by dogmatic-philosophical perception. If the world-soul is all that exists and Atman is its essence, then the idea of personality has to disappear. The shapeless All/One has been attained.

When this occurred, the Indian ceased to be creative; the dark, foreign blood of the Sudras—who were considered equal because of Atman—flowed in, annihilated the original concept of caste or race, and bastardization began. Snake and phallus cults began to fester among the natives. The symbolic expression of one-hundred-armed Siva became realistically represented as a fearful bastard-art developed in the primeval jungles. The old heroic odes were remembered only at the imperial court; only there could be found the lyrics of Kalidasa and other, mostly unknown, great poets. Cankara attempted to create Indian philosophy anew. It was in vain: the arteries of the race-body had been severed, and the Aryan-Indian blood flowed out, only here and there fertilizing the permeable soil of ancient India. Only a philosophical-technical doctrine was left behind for later life; and in its subsequent insanely distorted form this dominates contemporary Hindu life. We must not intolerantly maintain that the Indian gave up or perverted first his race and then his personality. Much more to the point is the metaphysical occurrence that was reflected in the passionate demand for the overthrow of the phenomenon of dualism, as well as the reciprocally-conditioning lower forms of this polarity.

Seen from the outside, philosophical recognition of the great equality of Atman-Brahman led to racial decline. In other lands such a phenomenon did not signify the solidification of a philosophical idea but was, rather, the consequence of uninterrupted miscegenation between two or many opposing races, whose respective capacities were neither elevated nor complemented by this process, but subjected to mutual annihilation.

... From the sixth century on, Iran experienced a great expansion on the part of the Aryan Persian. Under Arschama, there matured one of the leading religious teachers and great personalities of Indo-European history: Spitama (Zarathustra). Concerned over the fate of the Aryan minority, he formulated doctrines which, only today, are being revived in the West—insights concerning protection of the race, and demands for respect of kin.

However, since the ruling Aryan aristocracy lived in
scattered locales, Zarathustra had to transcend these
circumstances by creating an ideologically-bound community of belief. Ahura Mazda, the Eternal God of Light,
grew to the proportions of a cosmic idea—to being the
divine protector of the Aryan world. He had no abode
(although the Ancients and later the Romans provided
abodes for their gods); he is simply 'holy whiteness',
combining both completeness and humility. The dark
Angromayniu [Ahriman] stands opposed to him and, as
his enemy, battles with him for the domination of the
world. Here, Zarathustra posited a true, Nordic-Aryan
thought: in this struggle, man should fight on the side of
Ahura Mazda (just as the Einherjer were to fight for Odin
in Valhalla against the Fenris Wolf and the *Midgard-
schlange*).[3] Thus, a man should not lose himself in world-
shunning introspection or asceticism. Rather, he should
feel himself to be the struggling bearer of a world-
preserving idea, while awakening and strengthening all
the creative powers of the human soul. Whether he be a
thinker or one who makes the wilderness bloom, man
stands in the immediate service of the highest. He serves
and upholds the one creative principle wherever he goes—
whenever he sows and reaps; whenever he is true to
himself; and whenever he considers each hand-shake to be
an inviolable oath; as in the Vendidat, which expresses all
that is great and sublime in the phrase, 'Who sows grain,
sows holiness.'

However, evil and temptation lurk all around struggling

[3] From Nordic mythology. The Midgard Snake, the Fenris Wolf and
not mentioned here, Hel, goddess of death, were the three children of Loki,
god of evil, and the giantess Angur-Roda, portender of bad fortune. The
Einherjer were the souls of dead warriors who, with Thor, fought the giant
Midgard Snake, when he assaulted Valhalla. (Ed.)

mankind. In order to be able to oppose these forces effectively, Zarathustra calls upon Aryan blood. This call requires each Persian to serve the God of Light. After death, good and evil will be apportioned unto eternity. Ahura Mazda will defeat Angromayniu in a mighty struggle and construct his kingdom of peace.

For a time, the Persians drew their strength from this great religious poetry. But, in spite of these heroic efforts, the weakening of Aryan blood in Asia could not be avoided, and the great kingdom of the Persians declined. However, the spirit of Zarathustra and his *Mythus* exercised further influences upon the entire world. Judaism created its Satan from Angromayniu, and developed its own entirely artificial system of breeding a racial conglomeration from the Persian system of race preservation. This was combined with an obligation-ridden (of course, purely Jewish) religious law. The Christian Church appropriated the Persian saviour idea — which was embodied in Çaoshianç — for their prince of peace even though this had been distorted by Jewish messianic speculation. Today, with mysterious power, the same race-soul idea has been aroused to heightened consciousness in the northern heart of Europe. Even today, Nordic consciousness and Nordic racial-education represent the answer to the Syrian East which, in the form of Judaism and in many forms of raceless internationalism, has ensconced itself in Europe.

Persian civilization was a grafting upon the branch of Semitic-Oriental sub-strata. As business and money gained material influences for the trading races, and their representatives were allowed to attain power and high rank, this civilization began to disintegrate. Thus honour of kin vanished and the 'equalization' of all the races was consummated by the necessary form of bastardization.

A Persian king once had the following words chiselled upon the stone walls of Behisthun: I, DARIUS, GREAT KING AND KING OF KINGS OF THE ARYAN TRIBE ... Today, Persian mule-drivers pass unsuspectingly by these walls: a reminder for thousands that personality is both born and dies with race.

... The dream of Nordic humanity in Hellas was the most beautiful of all. Wave after wave came out of the Danube valley and deposited layers of ever-creative peoples upon those of the earlier Aryan and non-Aryan migrants. The ancient Mycenaean culture of the Achaean had already displayed an overwhelmingly Nordic character. Later, Dorian tribes again and again stormed the fortresses of the original inhabitants who were of a foreign race, enslaving the subjugated races and shattering the domination of the legendary Phoenician Semite King Minos. Until that time, he had controlled all of that world which later was to be called Greece. As rough masters and warriors, the Hellenic tribes supplanted the declining civilization of pre-Asiatic traders, and, together with the poorer classes of subjugated peoples, established a creative spirit beyond compare — sagas were created from stone and leisure time was utilized to compose and sing tales of eternal heroism. A true, aristocratic constitution prohibited miscegenation. Nordic strength, diminished by continual struggle, was continuously revived through sea migrations. Dorians and then Macedonians protected the creative blond blood until even these tribes were exhausted; then the overwhelming powers of Asia Minor infiltrated through a thousand channels, poisoned Hellas and, in place of the Greeks, deposited effete Levantines, who had only a name in common with their antecedents. The Hellenes had vanished for ever, and only dead images on stone, only a very few signs, testify to this heroic race-soul which once created Pallas Athene and Apollo. The total Nordic avoidance of magical forms is nowhere more clearly revealed than in the religious values of Greece, phenomena which too often have been ignored. Even when the investigator chooses to focus upon the religious side of Hellenic life, he all too often selects a period in which the Greek was already divided within himself, staggering back and forth between his own intrinsic values and those of a foreign spiritual realm. In contrast to this period, the earlier age of Homer, an age of fate-trusting majesty, constituted an epoch of true religiosity. The nineteenth century— itself an age of internal decline—was incapable of appreciating the Homeric mind, since this latter age of gold and silver did not rupture itself over 'ethical problems'. The figures of light—of Apollo, of Pallas Athene, of Zeus, the heavenly father—are signs of the truest and greatest piety. The golden-haired one (*chrysokomos*, Apollo) is the guardian and defender of everything noble and joyous, defender of order, instructor in the harmonizing of spiritual strengths, of artistic moderation. Apollo is the ascending light of dawn and, simultaneously, the guardian of internal perception and bringer of the gift of sight. He is the god of song and of rhythmic movement; not, however, of ecstatic dance. All that is holy was attributed to the god who emerged from the swan-ship of the North. He was a symbol of the bright (*Hellen*), of the majestic, and, in the style of the South, the palm is consecrated to him. The following phrases are engraved on the Delphic temples: ALL IN MODERATION, and KNOW THYSELF, two Homeric-Apollonian credos.

Next to Apollo there stands Pallas Athene, symbol of the life-giving lightning, who sprang from the head of Zeus, blue-eyed daughter of the thunderer, wise and discreet virgin and protectress of the Hellenic people in its struggles. These most pious creations of the Greek soul reveal the life of Nordic man, evenly developed and still pure. They are, in the highest sense, religious credos and expressions of a confidence in both the intrinsic character-istics of the Nordic spirit and in the deities who ingenuously revealed themselves as positively disposed towards men. 'Homer offers neither polemic nor dogma,' says Erwin Rohde* and in one sentence Rohde has described the essence of any truly religious feeling. Farther on, this profound student of the essence of Hellenism says, 'There is little of the innately portentous or ecstatic in Homer, and virtually no tendency in this direction.' It is the modera-tion of a superior race which resounds from the verses of the *Iliad* and which echoes in all the temples of Hellas. But beneath the creative ruling stratum, there lived and flourished Pelasgian, Phoenician, Alpine and, later, Syrian values; and the gods of these peoples pressed forward in direct proportion to the strengths of the respective races. If the Greek gods were heroes of light and heaven, the gods of the non-Aryans of Asia Minor bore all the mundane values. Demeter, Hermes and others are essential manifestations of this racial soul. If Pallas Athene was a warrior protectress in life struggle, the Pelasgian god Ares was the guardian of blood-smeared monstrousness. If Apollo was the god of the lyre and of song, Dionysus (at least in his non-Aryan aspect) was the god of ecstasy, of lust, of uninhibited frenzy.

*   *   *
* Rohde, *Psyche.*

As has been seen, Rosenberg traced the fall of the Hellenic world to the intrusion of non-Aryan Near-Eastern elements, as embodied in the new Chthonic gods. Moreover, the older masculine virtues gave way to lustful femininity. Racial miscegenation between the Aryan Greeks and barbarous Asians, standard-bearers of the mundane, brought disaster.

... After the miscegenation between Greeks and the earlier inhabitants, neither the Chthonic nor the heaven-bound elements developed in a pure form; rather, both elements were blended in Dionysian usages. At first, even Dionysus embodied the patriarchal principle. However, he degenerated into being the god of the dead (to whom Antigone also appealed). He lost the clean strong character of Apollo and became instead soft and besotted, finally sinking away into the daemonic maenadism of night. The animals that are consecrated to this god-daemon are those of darkness. These gods are born in hell and men pay homage to them only at night. Therefore, Dionysus entered into Greek life as something racially and spiritually foreign — even if we admit to his hoary past — and in this role he was a sure sign of the physical decline that accompanied the decline of the Nordic race. Under the flickering light of torches, accompanied by the clashing of metal cymbals, hand-clapping and the shrilling of flutes, Dionysian celebrants collect themselves into a swirling circle-dance. 'Mostly it was the women who whirled about in dance until exhaustion. They wore long flowing garments woven from fox pelts ... Their hair streamed wildly back; snakes, considered holy for the Sabbath, were held in their hands; they swung daggers ... In such a fashion did they rage until all their feelings were brought to peaks of excitement, and in "holy insanity" they fell upon the animals destined for sacrifice, clawing and tearing at the ceremonial beasts, and biting off the bloody flesh with their teeth they bolted it raw.'*

Each and every one of these customs was completely opposed to those of the Greeks. They represented that 'religion of frenzy' (Frobenius) which dominated the entire eastern region of the Mediterranean, a religion borne by the Afro-Asian races and race mixtures. We can draw a straight line from daemonic King Saul to the earth-bound lust of Dionysus (who was nevertheless ennobled by the Greeks), and finally to the whirling dervishes of later Islam.

The phallus became symbolic of the later 'Greek' conception of the world. This was not Greek, however. We can find no relationship between this and the salient aspects of Greek life and art. Rather, this was anti-Greek, Near-Eastern.

... The dramatic formation of Greece ... developed on two levels: on the one level we see an organic development of substance—from nature symbolism, crowned by the gods of light and the heavens, to Zeus, father of the gods: from the mystical-artistic level to dramatic-artistic recognition of these spiritual essences, and finally to the intellectual teachings of Plato, i.e. philosophical perception of the previously developed mythical-figurative forms. This entire chain of development, however, stands in continuous conflict with another blood-borne mythical and intellectual system. Part of this system was ennobled by being wedded to that of the Greeks. In the end, however, those systems which arose from the swamps of the Nile, the waters of Asia Minor and the wastes of Libya, rose up in opposition to the Nordic form of the Greeks

* Rohde, *Psyche.*

and sought to pervert, falsify and essentially annihilate its vital character.

However, this last phenomenon does *not* signify the explosion of natural tensions within an organic whole, but rather that dramatic struggle between two warring race-souls to which we bear transfixed witness today as we observe, with widened eyes, the decline of Hellas. Our blood dictates our position in this. Only bloodless scholars can call here for the 'parity of two great principles'.

With eternal sadness, we observe the epiphenomena of the psychic-racial decline of the Homeric Greeks, who once, in the proud words of the poet, entered the arena of world history 'To be always first and striving for change.' The race exhausted itself in struggles against the foe, against that disintegrating quality described by Theognis: that *money* mixes noble blood with that of the ignoble and that, in this manner, that race which is protected from asses and horses will become fouled by men. This view has its parallel in *Gorgias* where Plato vainly proclaims to the Callikles the wisest of all precepts: 'The law of nature demands that those of greatness rule over the lesser breeds.' To be sure 'our [Athenian] laws' were different: in accordance with them the most virtuous and the strongest, young as lions, are imprisoned and then misled by 'magical chantings and sophistries', by preachings of equality. However, if *one* of these people arises again he will brush aside these false rites and radiantly seek out the 'law of nature'. But this longing for the race's heroic men was in vain: money, and with it the *Untermensch*, already had triumphed over blood; without any direction the Hellenes began to become involved in trade, politics and philosophy, rejecting today what they had prized yesterday. Sons no longer respected their

fathers; slaves from all parts of the world called for
'freedom'; the equality of men and women was proclaimed. Symbolic of this democracy, the asses and horses
—as Plato scornfully remarked—began to press against
men, men who made no effort to avoid them. War
weakened the race as continuously new groups of the
population were accepted as citizens. 'For lack of men'
barbaric foreigners were accepted as 'Athenians', just as
Eastern Jews later would be accepted as 'German'
citizens. Thus, Isocrates remarked that after the Egyptian
expedition in A.D. 458 noble families who had endured the
Persian Wars had been exterminated. 'It is not in the best
interests of the city for it to accumulate at random citizens
from all ends of the earth, but only those who have best
preserved the race from the very beginning.' The significance of this could not have been any different than that
sorrowfully described by Jacob Burckhardt: 'Due to the
development of democracy, an uninterrupted persecution
of all meaningful individuals developed among the
Greeks ... The usual inexorable hatred against talent ...'*
However, this democracy was *not* the rule of the people,
but rather the domination of the Near East over the
Greek tribes, tribes whose manpower and strengths were
being rapidly dissipated. It was the rule of now-unin-
hibited scum over hoplites, who, no longer strengthened
through a racially-related peasantry, had become soft.
Unconscionable demagogues incited the masses against
the Romans in order to be able to denounce them later.
However, with the Roman advance there began a mass
flight from the threatened cities and poignant surrender
to the approaching masters, the slogan being, 'If we hadn't
declined so quickly, nothing could have saved us.' In the

* Jacob Burckhardt, *Griechische Kulturgeschichte*, vol. 4, p. 503.

maddened effort to 'reconstruct the law', the chaotic
democracy promulgated amnesties, pardons and land
divisions and in so doing became even more effete than
before.

The city-states exhausted themselves in bloody
economic struggles or became desolate or empty because
of the migrations of the Hellenes to all parts of the known
world. They either fertilized barbarian soil with culture or
underwent characteristic decline and physical annihilation.
Where flourishing cities once stood, where free Greeks
once battled in the arenas and shining temples once had
reflected a creative spirit, later travellers found desolate
ruins, depopulated land, fallen pillars. Only empty
pedestals remained as testimony to the statues of gods and
heroes that once had stood upon them. In Plutarch's
time it had been possible to raise up barely three thousand
hoplites and Dion Chrysostomus stated that the Ancient
Greek type had become a rather singular phenomenon:
'Does not the Pinios stream through an empty Thessally
and the Ladon[4] through a wasted Arcadia? ... Are there
now cities more devastated than Croton, Metapontum
and Tarentum?' Thus did Hysiäe, Tiryns, Asine and
Orneä lie in ruins; the temple of Zeus at Nemea had
fallen; even the port of Neapolis (Naples) was abandoned;
of the 'hundred cities' of Lacedaemon, a mere thirty
villages remained. Pausanias described the ruins of
Dorion and Andania in Mycenae. All that remained of
Pylos were ruins; of Leontim, only a few houses; the
'great city' (Megalopolis) in Arcadia was now only a
'great solitude'. Only a few miserable traces could be
found of Mantinea, Orchomenus, Heruä, Mänalos, Kyn-
ätha, etc., of Lycosura, only the town walls remained ...

[4] Rivers in Greece. (Ed.)

And yet even in decline the Greek had restricted the advance of Asia while scattering his brilliant gifts all over the world; gifts which assisted the Nordic Romans in nurturing a new culture, gifts which later became living legends for the German West. In spite of the sacrifice of the Greeks, Apollo still symbolized the first great triumph for Northern Europe, because behind him there emerged from new hyperborean depths bearers of the same values of psychic and spiritual freedom, organic life-contours and exploration of creative powers. For a long time the Roman sword dispelled the strengthened Near-Eastern apparition. More abruptly and more consciously than the Greeks, Rome nurtured the Apollonian parenthood principle, and through this strengthened both state-thinking itself and the institution of marriage, pre-conditions for *Volk* and race preservation. The Romans served in this capacity until the Germans, in an ever newer form, became the representatives of the god of heaven.*

* From time to time one comes across this point of view in Rohde's wonderful work *Psyche*. It is true that Rohde is focusing only upon the chaotic period of late Hellenism when he speaks of 'insane rites from all parts of the world' from 'the most foreign ... nuisance of excommunication' to the 'babble of foreign idols and base daemonic powers'. However, his whole work forthrightly demands an investigation as to how these pre-Greek primeval strengths—which are mentioned much earlier in the work—were depicted, accepted or overthrown. *Today*, he certainly would not hesitate to declare that the Python which was buried 'under the navel-stone of the earth-goddess' was the 'Chthonic daemon' of the ancient Near-Eastern god whose functions Apollo took over to the degree that he was unable to overthrow him. Erochtheus 'dwelling in the temple', similarly represents the figure of a foreign race-souls. It speaks well for Rohde's genial lack of bias when he somewhat grievously remarks that, 'the continuously deeper penetration of an anxious timidity before invisibly efficacious spiritual powers, a superstition such as Homer's age had never known, was based upon powers attributed to the later oracles.' Furthermore, the mixture of the Greek hero cult with the Chthonic gods would appear to Rohde today as a compromise resulting from the dramatic clashing of two different race-souls. Therefore, his whole work is a confirmation of the race-soul *Weltanschauung*

... The history of Rome bears marked similarities to that of Greece, but it is set against a broader expanse of territory and greater political-power structures. Rome was also established through a Nordic migration which had broken the domination of the Etruscan – this 'obscure' foreign (Near-Eastern) people – long before the Germanen and Galliern gushed into the fruitful valleys south of the Alps. Presumably a marriage was then contracted with the still pure tribes of inbred middle-Mediterranean races, and this marriage begat a Nordic-shaped character of great firmness and toughness. This new Nordic man embodied all the virtues of master, farmer and hero wedded to a judicious sense and an iron energy. Ancient Rome, of which history knows very little, became a true *Volk* state through racial breeding and that plain character obtained through and necessitated by the struggle against collective Orientalism. All the brains and power which would later be squandered when Rome entered into world conflicts were formed and accumulated in this prehistoric age. The ruling three hundred noblemen supplied the three hundred senators from whom province leaders and field-marshals were drawn. Surrounded by the seafaring races of the Near East, Rome often had to use its short sword with ruthlessness in order to defend itself. The destruction of Carthage was a deed of great importance in

---

as it has been born today. One can also read of this viewpoint in Fustel de Coulanges's *La Cité Antique,* and above all in Burckhardt's imperishable *Griechische Kulturgeschichte,* whose data on racial-spiritual separation have attained peculiar significance and meaning only today. [The Erochtheum is one of the most well-known buildings on the Acropolis. It was completed during the latter portions of the 5th century B.C. and was dedicated to Erochtheus, ancestral god of Attica. When Rosenberg refers to the influence of the 'later oracles', he, of course, is referring to what he saw as the intrusion of Eastern superstition into the Hellenic world after the 5th century B.C. (Ed.)]

race history; because of this even the later cultures of Central and Western Europe were spared from the breath of this Phoenician pestilence. World history might well have taken another course had the destruction of Carthage been accompanied by the completely successful destruction of all other Near-Eastern, Semitic-Jewish centres. The act of Titus came too late, however; the Near-Eastern parasite no longer dwelt in Jerusalem itself, but had already extended its strongest tentacles from Egypt and 'Hellas' to Rome itself. And this occurred in Rome as well. Everybody who was possessed by ambition and lust for profit was drawn to the capital city on the Tiber and there made great efforts, through promises and gifts, to induce the 'sovereign', self-governing *Volk* to acquiesce in their decisions. Through the efforts of these foreign immigrants, there arose from the earlier plebiscite —which consisted of people equal before the law and with common roots and characteristics—a degraded mass of humanity without conscience which constituted a permanent threat to the state. Cato later stood like a lonely rock in this quagmire. As praetor of Sardinia, consul of Spain and finally as censor in Rome he fought against corruption, usury and wasteful extravagance. In this he was similar to the other Cato who, after fruitless struggles to prevent the utter decay of the state, plunged a sword into himself. This deed has been called old Roman. Certainly it was. However, Ancient old Roman traits are essentially Nordic in character. When the later Germans offered their services to emperors who were weak, degenerate and surrounded by impure bastards, they were attesting to the same spirit of honour and loyalty that had been manifested in the Ancient Roman. The Emperor Vitellius, a coward without peer, was surprised in his hiding-place by enemies who dragged him about the Forum by a rope tied around his neck. However, his German bodyguard did not surrender. They were bound by oath to fight to the last man. This was that Nordic spirit shared in common by Cato and the Germans. We saw it again in Flanders in 1914, at the Coronel Islands, and for years throughout the world.

By the middle of the fifth century the first steps towards chaos had been taken; mixed marriages between patricians and plebeians were legalized. For Rome, as for Persia and Hellas, mixed marriages signified the collapse of *Volk* and state. In A.D. 336, the first plebeians had already pushed their way into the Roman Assembly and around the year A.D. 300, there were reports of plebeian priests. In A.D. 287, the plebeian public assembly had been elevated to the position of being a state institution. Tradesmen and money-changers hawked their wares; ambitious apostate priests like the Gracchi, driven perhaps by a generous but falsely presented sense of benevolence, displayed democratic tendencies.[5] Others, such as Publius Claudius, openly placed themselves at the head of Roman city mobs.

Only a few stood out in these times of chaos: blue-eyed, powerful Sulla, and the pure Nordic head of Augustus. However, they could not stand in the way of fate. And so it happened that leadership of the Roman masses—and this meant rule over a truly huge Empire—became transformed into a monstrous game of chance, i.e. who ruled the praetorian guard or was able to lead a mass of hungry men. At one time, a truly great individual would arise; at another time, a bloodhound. Rome's formerly

[5] Here Rosenberg displays some confusion. The Gracchi were prominent in the 2nd century B.C., i.e. in Republican Rome.

powerful racial forces were utterly exhausted in the
course of four hundred years of race-destroying democracy.
The rulers of Rome now came from the provinces.
Trajan was the first Spaniard to achieve the purple,
Hadrian the second. This 'empire by adoption' originated
as a last attempt to preserve the state. It arose from the
feeling that since no trust could be placed in blood any
more, the state could preserve itself only through personal
selection. The values of Marcus Aurelius, who was also a
Spaniard, had already been weakened through the
introduction of Christianity, and he openly elevated
protection of slaves, the emancipation of women and
assistance to the poor (today we call it unemployment
benefit) to being principles of the state. He also dis-
franchised the *paterfamilias*, which had been the strongest.
tradition of republican Rome and which was the only
source of type formation still extant. There then followed
Septimius Severus, an African. 'Enrich the soldiers; despise
all others,' he advised his sons Caracalla and Geta. Under
the influence of his Syrian mother (daughter of a priest of
Baal in Asia Minor), Caracalla, this loathsome bastard
who also sat on the throne of Caesars, declared that all
'free' inhabitants of the Roman region were citizens.

This was the end of the Roman world. Macrinus then
murdered Caracalla and himself became Emperor. After
he was killed he was succeeded by the monster Elagabal,
nephew of the African Severus. In the midst of all this,
there arose the half-German Maximinus 'Thrax' and
Philippus 'The Arab', a Semite. Often, only non-Romans
lounged about on the senate seats. The 'culture' of this
epoch was supplied by Martial, a Spaniard, the Greeks
Plutarch, Strabo and Dio Cassius, etc. Apollodorus, who
expanded the Forum, was also a Greek.

Aurelian, who **was** an Illyrian born in Belgrade, was included in this last category, as was Diocletian, who was also Illyrian, born of a slave (perhaps of half-German ancestry) and heir to the throne of the Caesars. Constantius Chlorus also came from Illyria, but was of more elevated extraction. After his death, the legionaries selected a truly mighty man to bear the title Augustus: Constantine, the son of Constantius Chlorus and a barmaid from Bithynia. Constantine was victorious over all his rivals. At this point the history of Imperial Rome ends and that of papal and Germanic Rome begins.

Roman, Near-Eastern, Syrian, African and Greek elements were all mixed together in this bewildering diversity. The gods and mortals of all lands appeared on the venerable Forum. Priests of Mithras sacrificed their bulls upon it, while latter-day Greeks prayed to Helios. Astrologers and Oriental conjurers boasted of their miracles. The 'Emperor' Elagabal harnessed six white horses to a gigantic meteor stone and had this drawn through the streets of Rome as the image of Baal of Emesa. He himself danced at the head of the procession. All the ancient gods were dragged along behind him, and the 'people' of Rome rejoiced at the spectacle. The senators yielded. Ballad-singers and barbarians rose to positions of senator or consul. Finally, even Elagabal was strangled and thrown into the Tiber, which had served as a final resting-place for thousands for two millennia. Newer racial-historical investigation aside, this interpretation of Roman history would have been necessary, because in studying Ancient Roman customs, definitions of law and of state—in *all* areas—we observe those hoary values which were closely related to African-Near-Eastern ones, gradually or suddenly transformed into their opposites, even if they preserved their former names. From this our learned historians 'ascertain'—and they are still doing so even today—that Etruscans, Sabines, Oskers, Sabellians, Aequi and Samnites lived in northern and central Italy, while Phoenicians, Siculers, Near-Eastern people and Greek settlers and traders lived in the south.[6] And suddenly, we don't know how or why, a struggle broke out against a portion of these tribes and people; a struggle against its gods and goddesses, against its concepts of law, against its political pretensions. No mention is made of the new *bearers* of this struggle, or if perchance there is, no one inquires as to their essence. In this context the scholarly world helps out with the famous phrase 'development of humanity', which is interjected for purposes of 'ennoble-ment'. Here the fact collectors are at one with their opponents, the romantic interpreters of myth, that the Etruscan certainly possessed a 'higher culture' than the bucolic Latin. Since this concept of a sudden, almost magi-cal 'development' towards higher forms of spirituality and government has been discredited, in time new interpreters of history established the so-called culture-circle theory [*Kulturkreislehre*], a phrase which is every bit as devoid of content as that other exclusive belief, 'general develop-ment', a term which also is encountered only in the brain of scholar or priest. This is naturally so because just as little is said of the *creators* of the culture-circles as had been in the works of nineteenth-century papists of evolution. One fine day such a circle, be it Indian, Persian, Chinese or Roman, descends upon a particular region, and thanks to its magical touch, induces a complete transformation in

[6] Rosenberg here is throwing together a number of tribes and groups of people who lived in Italy before the advent of Rome. He is attempting to show how such phenomena as culture-borrowing and assimilation have no role to play in a racial scheme of history. (Ed.)

the character of a similar group of human beings who, until touched by the circle, had embraced certain customs. Then we learn of the 'biological' growth, maturation and decline of this magical circle, until, because of violent criticism, the theoreticians of this 'morphology of history' finally mumble something about blood and blood relationships around the second or third volume.

Even this new intellectualistic obscurantism is beginning to disappear. The 'Roman culture-circle', the 'new development', did not stem from the creativity of native Etruscan-Phoenician blood, but originated *in opposition* to this blood and its values. The bearers of these new values were Nordic emigrants and Nordic warriors who, on Italian soil, began to displace the Ligurians, the primeval Negroid race (which originated in Africa) and the Near-Eastern Etruscans. Certainly this Nordic race had to make many concessions to the region. However, in the most bitter of struggles it held fast to its innate character and, more ruthlessly than the more refined Hellenes, pressed it forward (as exemplified in the driving out of the last Etruscan king, Tarquinius Superbus). Many of these accomplishments remained as a common heritage for all Europe. However, the foaming waves of race-chaos remained high and they bore into Europe much that was decayed and alien.

Therefore, the Etruscans, Ligurians, Sikales, Phoenicians (primarily Carthaginians), did not represent 'earlier levels of development'; they were not 'tribes of the Roman people' in which each contributed to the 'general cultural advancement' of the other. Rather the builders of the Roman state stood opposed to these peoples on the basis of racial-*Volkish* principles, subdued them and over a period of time destroyed them. Only that spirit, that will, those

values which were given form in this *struggle*, deserved to
be called Roman. The Etruscans offer a typical example
of the fact that non-Aryan peoples could not improve
upon or ennoble the Greek cultural base. Just like other
Near-Eastern peoples, they had first discovered the
Atlantic-Nordic myths, then they attempted as best they
could to imitate Greek symbolic and art forms, exprop-
riating even the Hellenic Olympus. Yet they succeeded
only in corrupting all that they touched, in turning each
attribute into its opposite. This provides reason enough for
the sympathy which, even today, is displayed by certain
'researchers' for the 'extraordinary spiritual heritage' of
the Etruscans, as well as for the 'basis for growth' they
provided and for the 'world-historical consecration'
symbolized by their 'tragic fate';* reason enough, since
ascending asphalt humanity of the metropolis is bound in a
very definite manner to all the refuse of Asia ...

* * *

Rosenberg concluded his critique of the ancient world by indicating
that those barbarians who represented Asia, the Etruscans,
contributed to the rise of the papacy. The latter simply absorbed
the role that had been assigned to the barbaric Haruspices, the
Etruscan priests and diviners of the savage mother goddess.

The Haruspices were victorious. The Roman papacy
arose as their immediate successor, while the temple hierarchy, the College of Cardinals, represented a blend of
the Etrusco-Syrian-Near-Eastern priesthood and the Jews,
with the Nordic Roman senate. Thus, 'our' medieval
Weltanschauung went back to the Etruscan Haruspices,
particularly that fearful superstition regarding witchcraft,

* For example, Hans Mühlestein, *Die Geburt des Abendlandes* (Berlin,
1928).

in whose name millions of Europeans were sacrificed; a belief which did not die out with the *Hexenhammer*,[7] but which lives on today in Church literature, ready to be brought forth again. Traces of this can be seen in the forms of those apparitions which, not infrequently, disfigure Nordic-Gothic cathedrals and which go somewhat beyond natural grotesqueness. Etruscan-bastardized antiquity lives on in grandiose style even in Dante:* in the *Inferno*, with its ferryman of hell and the fiery swamps of the Styx; in the bloody, Pelasgian Erinyes and Furies; in the Cretan Minotaur; in those daemons in the form of disgusting birds who torment suicides, and in the amphibious monstrosity, Geryon. The damned must run under a rain of fire in a burning wasteland, while evil-doers are transformed into bushes which spit out blood and eternal cries as Harpies gnaw upon them — cries of agony as each branch is broken. Black bitches race behind the damned, tearing at them and adding to their fearful torment; horrid devils scourge the swindlers, and prostitutes are sunk into stinking excrement. Sunk into holes, there languish the simony-tarnished popes themselves, their writhing feet outlined in painful flames; Dante cries out accusingly against the degenerate papacy, the whore of Babylon.

---

[7] A document *Malleus Malificarum* written by two papal Inquisitors, Heinrich Institoris and Jacob Sprenger, in 1489. Rapid assimilation of the work led to new outbreaks of persecution. (Ed.)

* Perhaps we can even single out here the figure of Machiavelli. Although he fought against the Church for a national Italian state, his school of political thought was based upon a view of politics that believed in fundamental truths valid for all time. Also, his view was predicated upon an acceptance of human baseness and a *fundamental dedication* to it that could not have emerged from the Nordic soul. Machiavelli came from the port of Montespertoli which, as his biographer Giuseppe Prezzolini declares in *Das Leber Nicolo Macciavellis* (deutsch. Dresden, 1929) 'had a predominantly Etruscan character'.

The tomb-markings in Tuscany reveal that all these representations of the underworld are Etruscan. We see depicted, just like in the medieval 'Christianized' upper world, the hands of hanged men tortured with blazing faggots and other implements of martyrdom—and this is given as a representation of Eternity. The Etruscans depicted the murdering, vengeful Furies as 'hateful through and through, with animalistic or negroid facial features, pointed ears, hair hanging in clusters, fangs and so on'.* In such a manner did one bird-beaked Fury use her poisonous tongue to torture Theseus (does this reveal a primeval hatred of the legendary conquerer of the ancient nightmare of Athens?), as can be seen represented in the wall-paintings of the Tomba dell'Orico at Corneto. Besides these figures, hideous male and female daemons of death named Typhon and Echidna are at work—they are shown as having legs and hair of snakes and as being one-eyed. Moreover, with sadistic care the Etruscans dwelt upon every possible representation of suffering, murder and sacrifice—human slaughter was especially exciting to them.

Musically untalented, in essence completely unpoetic, incapable of producing an organic architecture of their own and not possessing the rudiments of a true philosophy, this Near-Eastern people dedicated itself with great perseverance to examining the entrails of birds, and to complicated magical and sacrificial rites. Also, it was almost totally committed to commerce, and because it was resilient and tough it poisoned Roman blood, while its terrifying representations of hellish suffering in the world to come were transmitted to the Church. The most monstrous animal and human daemons have become

* Müller-Deecke, *Die Etrusker*, vol. II, page 109.

permanent tools of the papacy, and through the world of imagination that had been poisoned by the Roman Church these monstrosities dominated our Middle Ages— the painting of the period alone testifies to this. Evidence for this can be found even on the Isenheim Altar, to say nothing of the excursions into hell undertaken by others in the plastic arts. Only when we have learned to discern the foreign nature of this world, have become conscious of its sources and have brought to the fore that will to resist which is necessary in order to exorcize this fearful apparition—only then will we have overcome the 'Middle Ages'. Through this the Roman Church, which is for ever bound to the agonies of the Etruscan underworld, will collapse from within.

It is thus that the whole fearful mythology of Dante's *Inferno* presents a shocking representation of ancient Etruscan, Near-Eastern Satanism combined with Christianity. However, even though Dante was held in the embrace of a thousand-year-old daemonology, the German spirit stirred itself in him.*

In *Purgatory*, Virgil says the following about Dante, 'He is searching for freedom.' This was a statement which contradicted that spiritual world from which representations of devils and witches had arisen. Finally, Virgil is

* We are now certain that Dante was of German ancestry. He was called Dante Aldiger, which is a pure Germanic name. Dante's father was the great-grandson of Cacciaguida, who was mentioned in the *Divine Comedy* and who, under Conrad III, participated in the Crusades and was dubbed a knight by the Emperor himself. His wife was a woman who came from the old Germanic race of the Aldiger. All his life Dante had testified to that aspect of Nordic thought which called for independence of earthly powers from the domination of priests, i.e. he made common cause with the Ghibellines. He did not shrink from placing the degenerate popes in hell and from calling Rome a sewer. Above all he composed his poetry in the language of the *Volk*, to whom he dedicated a special essay which was also an argument against abstract Latin.

able happily to leave his charge, since the latter has
satisfactorily acquired his own strength:

My knowledge, my word, can do no more for thee;
Freedom, temperateness, healthiness are the marks of thy will
Most foolish would he be who did not yield to it.

These are the two worlds that tore the heart of northern medieval man: the Near-Eastern description of
the horrible underworld, a fearful one nurtured by
the Church, and the longing to be 'free, temperate and
healthy'. The German can be creative only to the degree
that he is free, and centres of European culture developed only where the insane belief in witches did not
prevail.

Into this Rome, one that had matured into racelessness,
came Christianity. It brought with it a concept that to a
great extent makes its victory understandable: the teaching of the sinful nature of the world and the preaching
of grace which was its natural complement. A people who
possessed an unbroken race-character would have been
unable to understand the doctrine of original sin, for in
such a people there dwells a secure confidence in itself and
in its expressed Will, which is taken as Fate. Homer's
heroes knew as little about 'sin' as did the ancient Indians
and the Germans of Tacitus and the tales of Dietrich.
Opposed to this, an enduring sense of sin is a betraying
mark of physical bastardization. Race-crime is revealed in
several ways: in an aimlessness in thinking and acting; an
inner uncertainty—the feeling that existence is simply the
'wages of sin' and not the mysterious and necessary
task of self-development. This feeling of depravity arouses
a longing for grace, the only hope for an existence
characterized by race-crime. Therefore it was natural that

anyone who still possessed character turned against the rising Christianity, all the more so since these religious teachings also represented a thoroughly proletarian nihilistic *political* trend. The bloody persecutions of Christians that took place were not, as Church history would have it, suppressions of conscience (the Forum was free to all gods), but rather the suppression of an event which was seen as a political threat to the state. For the purpose of annihilating the spirit, the Church, in its Pauline-Augustinian form, preserved doctrinal councils, the Inquisition and the stake.

Classical-Nordic antiquity could not abide this sort of thing and the German world also had rebelled against the Syrian characteristics.

... Christianity, as it was introduced into Europe through the Roman Church, goes back to many sources. This is not the place to examine them but rather to make but a few observations.

As the Church has depicted it, the great personality of Jesus Christ has been burdened with all the sterility of Near-Eastern, Jewish and African life. In Asia Minor the Romans exercised a stern rule and, from necessity, they enforced taxation. The hopes of the oppressed peoples became centred upon a leader of slaves and a liberator: this was the legend of *Christos*. From Asia Minor the legend travelled to Palestine, where it became organically linked with Jewish messianic speculation and where it finally became transferred to the personality of Jesus. The maxims and precepts of Near-Eastern prophets were passed off as Jesus' own preachings, paradoxically enough, in order to outbid the old Aryan requirements. For example, we see that the Jews already had appropriated the nine-commandment system as *their* ten commandments.* Thus Galilee became tied to all of Syria and Asia Minor. The Christian movement—which had stirred up the older forms of life—appeared to the Pharisee Paul to hold great promise as well as usefulness. In a sudden decision he converted to it and, girding himself in unrestrained fanaticism, he preached international revolution against the Roman Empire. In spite of all efforts at accommodation, his teachings still constitute the Jewish-spiritual foundation as well as the Talmudic-Oriental side of both the Catholic and Lutheran Churches. Paul accomplished something which is never admitted in Church circles: he made the Jewish national uprising internationally effective, while allowing for the still further spread of racial chaos in the ancient world. The Jews in Rome knew very well why their synagogues were placed at his disposal for purposes of proselytizing. That Paul himself (in spite of occasional criticism of the Jews) was quite conscious that he represented Jewish interests, can be seen in several candid references in his letters.

' ... that blindness in part is happened to Israel shall be saved, those who are loved for the fathers' sake. Who are Israelites; to whom *pertaineth* the adoption, and the glory and the covenants, and the giving of the law, and the service of *God*, and the promises...and of whom as concerning the flesh Christ came ... For if thou wert cut out of the olive tree which is wild by nature, and wert graffed contrary to nature into a good olive tree: how much more shall these, which be the natural *branches*, be graffed onto their own olive tree?'[8]

* Erbt, *Weltgeschichte auf rassischer Grundlage.*
[8] Rom. 11 :25; 9 :4, 5; 11 :24. The translation given here is taken from the King James Version. (Ed.)

The evangelical teachings of St John which were still imbued throughout with the aristocratic spirit, attempted to defend Christianity against this collective bastardization, Orientalization and Judaification. Around A.D. 150, there arose the Greek, Markion, who, on behalf of Nordic thought introduced a cosmology which was based upon organic tension and hierarchy. This was done in opposition to the Semitic image of the arbitrary power of God and his limitless domain of power. Here he also condemned the 'Book of Laws' of so false a God, i.e. the so-called Old Testament. Several of the Gnostics also attempted to do this. However, thanks to racial disintegration Rome had allied itself with Africa and Syria, had discarded the straightforward personality of Jesus and had fused the later-Roman ideal of world Empire with the conception of a nationless world Church.

The struggles of the first century after Christ can be seen as being nothing other than the struggles of several race-souls against Hydra-headed race chaos. In this, the Syrian-Near-Eastern adaptation, with its superstitions, insane magic and sensual 'mysticism', gathered behind all that was chaotic, broken and degenerate, and impressed upon Christianity that schismatic character from which it still suffers. In this way a servile religion pressed into Europe, shielded, as it were, by the misused great personality of Jesus.* The appearance of Christianity,

* As far as Jesus' ancestry is concerned, there is not the slightest reason to believe, as Chamberlain and Delitzsch have already explained, that Jesus was of Jewish ancestry, even if it be admitted that He had grown up in Jewish intellectual circles. One can find several interesting, if only hypothetical, suggestions in Dr E. Jung's *Die geschichtliche Persönlichkeit Jesu* (München, 1924). We will probably never be able to ascertain scientifically the ancestry of Jesus. We must content ourselves with recognizing the probability of His non-Jewish ancestry. The thoroughly un-Jewish teachings of the 'kingdom of heaven within us' strengthen this realization.

which drew nourishment from many sources, points out
with special effectiveness the curious inner relationship
between abstract spirituality and daemonic magic, not-
withstanding other streams that were assimilated by it.
For example, the idea of the trinity was known to many
peoples of the Middle-Eastern region in the form of
father, mother, son, and further in the perception that
'Everything is divided three ways' (the aggregate condition of the primary substances). The mother symbolized
the fertile earth, the father, the generative light principle.
In place of the mother there now appeared the 'Holy
Ghost' in conscious rejection of the purely physical—of
the *hagion pneuma* of the Greeks, of the *Prâna* of the Indians.
However, this accented spirituality was not embedded
in a racial-*Volkish* type; it was not determined according
to polarities, by an *organic life*. Rather it developed into
a power that despised all races. Paul wrote to the Galatians
(the last remnant of a great Celtic migration from the
Danube valley to Asia Minor), 'There is neither Jew nor
Greek, there is neither bond nor free, there is neither
male nor female.' On the basis of this nihilism he called for
a belief in Christ which belies everything organic. This
represented a complete reversal of the culture-creative
values of Greece and Rome although to be sure, Christianity embodied these values in a degenerate form and
through its exclusiveness was finally able to gather around
it all those who had lost direction.

A further step towards the demise of natural union
occurred in the *dogmatic assertion* of the Virgin Birth—a
phenomenon that can be found among all peoples from
the South Sea Islands to Northern Europe as a permuta-
tion of the sun myth.

This abstract spirituality was flanked, however, by all

the sorceries of Asia Minor, Syria and Africa: the demons
that were driven out by Jesus and assumed the form of
pigs; the stormy waters which were stilled at His command; His 'witnessed' Resurrection and journey to
heaven after a martyr's death—all of these represented
the peculiar 'factual' point of departure for Christianity,
and it no doubt allowed for great endurance in the face of
suffering. Thus, the world was not elevated because of the
life of the Saviour, but because of His *death* and its miraculous consequences. This is the sole motif of the Pauline
Scriptures. Goethe, however, feeling the *life* of Christ to
be important and not His death, thereby attested to the
soul of the German West—*positive* Christianity, as opposed
to *negative* Christianity, which was founded upon a priesthood and witch-mania that went back to Etrusco-African
beliefs.

* * *

*As was so often the case, Rosenberg wasted no time in attempting to
put the travails of Christianity in historical context. This context
was the fall of Rome to new Germanic hordes—replenished in
Volk spirit—and the subsequent birth of the Middle Ages, when
the Church used German against German. In this discussion,
Rosenberg pays homage to the perverse genius of Houston Stewart
Chamberlain.*

Negative and positive Christianity are in eternal conflict, and this battle is being waged more bitterly today
than ever before. The negative variety rests upon its
surrender to Syrian-Etruscan elements, upon abstract
dogmas and hoary customs; the positive variety
consciously summons to life the powers of Nordic blood, as

did the first Germans when they once pressed into Italy, bequeathing new life to this sickly land.

The storm of the Cimbern from the north broke like a threatening primitive force of fate. Defences could no longer prevent the Nordic Celts and Germans from again and again threatening the borders of Rome. One campaign after another revealed that the usual Roman tactics could not prevail against the rough-and-ready power of the Germans. Giant blond 'slaves' appeared in Rome, and the German beauty ideal became fashionable in a degenerate *Volkstum* deprived of all ideals. Free Germans were no longer an oddity in Rome, and gradually the loyalty of the German soldier became the strongest protection of the Caesars. However, at the same time they constituted the most threatening danger to the state, which had become poor in spirit and in values. Augustus attempted to increase the number of 'his' people by punishing bachelors, subsidizing marriages and public welfare. It was in vain. Germans were making their influence felt in the selection of Claudius, of Galba and of Vitellius. Marcus Aurelius dispatched his German prisoners from Vienna to Italy and, instead of making them gladiators, had them farm the desolate Ancient Roman soil. Actually by the time of Constantine the whole Roman army had become German. Whoever is unable to perceive here the efficacy of racial strength, must truly be blind to any phenomena of historical development. We can almost feel decomposition and rebirth; a rebirth which then extended past Constantine to include Stilicho, Alaric, Ricimer, Odoacer, Theodoric, the Langobardi, the Normans—who erected a kingdom from the south on up—to the inconceivably great Frederick II of the Hohenstaufens, who formed the first secular state, the

Sicilian royal house, and who settled its provinces with German aristocrats.[9]

In the history of the Nordic rule of Italy the figure of Theodoric the Great stands out prominently. For over thirty years this strong and yet gentle and generous man ruled over the Roman Empire. What Marcus Aurelius and Constantine had begun, he advanced further: Germans were no longer only tenant and small farmers; they now became large landowners—a third of all occupied land went over into the hands of pure, Germanic soldiery. Although unfortunately dispersed, over two hundred thousand German farmers were settled in Tuscany, Ravenna and Venetia. Once again, German farmers drew ploughs through the soil of northern central Italy. They made formerly sterile soil fruitful again and independent from North African grain imports. Set apart by marriage laws and by the Aryan belief in 'the innate', the Goths (and later the Langobardi) undertook the same character-building tasks as had the first Nordic migrants, the ones who once had built republican Rome. Racial miscegenation began only with conversion to Catholicism. In the end, the Renaissance itself developed as a thunderous reaffirmation of Nordic, this time German, blood. Here, in a sudden shattering of previously-sanctioned social bonds, one genius after another sprang up from cultivated soil; while all of Africanized southern Italy from Rome on down remained mute and uncreative, at least until today when Fascism—again northern-based —is attempting to awaken anew the old values. *Attempting*!

For a long time, the notion had been current that all

[9] These are all German rulers who exercised great influence in Italy between the 5th and 13th centuries. (Ed.)

Western states and their respective creative values had been produced by the Germans. However, the necessary conclusion, later drawn by H. S. Chamberlain, had not yet been established. This man attained the insight that with the complete disappearance of German blood in Europe (and also the gradual evaporation of the nation-creating strengths procreated by this blood) all of Western culture would have to go with it. The new investigations of prehistory as consummated by Chamberlain, combined with racial studies, have brought forth an even deeper inner reflection: the fearful awareness that today we stand before a *final* decision; either we attain, through a re-experiencing and cultivation of primal blood combined with an elevated will to struggle, a new purifying level of achievement, or even the last Germanic-Western values of civilization and state discipline will vanish amidst filthy metropolitan crowds, crippled upon the hot, barren asphalt of a bestialized inhumanity or trickling away, in the form of a self-bastardizing emigration, as a sickness-inducing germ, to South America, China, the Dutch Indies and Africa.

Besides his emphasis upon a new world-basis through *Germanentum*, another basic idea of H. S. Chamberlain today appears as being of decisive significance: that another epoch is inserting itself between the one of Old-Nordic-conditioned Rome and the new one of a German-shaped West, an epoch which will be character-ized by limitless racial mixing, i.e. bastardization. A total world crisis will result from this stirring-up of all that has been sickened by excessive ecstasies, bloated Syrian superstitions and the fevered state of all humanity. Chamberlain labels this age with a title reflective of the true, history-making artist: the age of *Volk*-chaos. Even if this cannot be precisely fixed in time this designation of a certain condition has become general knowledge today, the self-evident heritage of all possessed of deep perception. This new heuristic principle in place of 'ancient times' and 'Middle Ages' was, in the highest sense of the word, one of the greatest discoveries in terms of life-laws and spiritual lore of the vanishing nineteenth century, a discovery which has become the basis of our own historical observations of the progressing twentieth century. For this precept signifies that if no Theodoric had followed Caracalla 'eternal night' would have spread its wings over Europe. The bloated, oozing flood of Asian, African and Mediterranean half-breeds probably would have settled down after much vacuous excitement; constant upheavals would very probably have exterminated many of the putrefied and crippled. But the creative strength of a continuously self-procreating soul would have been lost for ever, as would the earth-shaping genius of Nordic men—the explorers of the universe. Only a low-grade humanity would have preserved a vegetable-like existence, much as is still the case in southern Italy, not living, but, in a crippled condition, frittering itself away, without bold energy of body and soul, dwelling without desire in most submissive contentment on lava masses or amidst stony wastes.

Therefore, if even today, around two thousand years after the appearance of the Germans, there still exist somewhere national cultures, creative strengths and a daring spirit of adventure, these forces—even if they still fight among themselves—owe their entire beings solely to the new Nordic wave which streamed in stormy tides over all of Europe and beyond, inundating and bearing fruit as it spilled to the foot of the Caucasus and surged past the pillars of Hercules, only to perish in the wastes of North Africa.

Seen in terms of major patterns of development, all of European history consists of a struggle between this new humanity and the forces of Roman *Volk*-chaos which, numbering in the millions, stretched from the Danube to the Rhine.

This dark wave carries conspicuous values upon its surface and provides nerve-tingling lusts; its billows speak of a past once-mighty, world domination and of a world religion that answers all questions. A great portion of Nordic blood, carefree and with childish dissipation, surrendered itself to the captivating enticement; it even became the bearer of a half-imaginary Ancient Roman grandeur. All too often they drew their swords over the entire world in the service of a phantasy, and instead of filling their hereditary role as *ancestors*, they became simple *inheritors*. In such a manner, until Martin Luther, did the struggle between *Germanentum* and *Volk*-chaos take form: it became a struggle between a nature-bound heroism and another heroism, imprisoned in the service of an unnatural phantasy. It was not unusual to find that those who stood facing each other, weapon in hand, in defence of respective, mortally-opposed values, were of the *same blood*.

* * *

The Middle Ages were thus a time of tragedy for the unhappily ingenuous German soul. Its heroic virtues were misused by the Near-Eastern-Syrian Roman Church. Furthermore, even the sixteenth century, although it brought Martin Luther to the fore (Rosenberg's attitudes towards him will be revealed at a later time) was an age of tragedy for the Aryan race. Its influence in France was wiped out with the Nordic Huguenots. From the massacre of St Bartholomew on, France degenerated into the temporal Whore of Babylon of the twentieth century.

The decisive fact that emerges from this blood-bath [the persecution of the Huguenots in the sixteenth century] *is the alteration of the character of the French nation.* That true pride, that inflexibility and noble courage that was embodied in the Huguenot leadership was lost for ever. When 'classical' French philosophy in the seventeenth and eighteenth centuries began again to undermine and bring down Church dogma, it was certainly endowed with great sharpness and splendid wit. However—this can be seen with Rousseau and even with Voltaire—it was lacking in that great nobility of spirit of the kind which Bequin honoured in a Condé, Coligny[10] or Téligny. However, even what spirituality there was was inwardly lacking in life and soul; and so, July 14th, 1789, was a manifestation of characteristic impotence. By 1793 the French Revolution which, under Coligny, had been a true and vital one, had become a merely bloody one, besides being devoid of any substance. This was so because it was not led by anyone of greatness. The Girondists and Jacobins inspired no geniuses, but only raving philistines, vain demagogues and those hyenas of political battlefields who rob the abandoned of their belongings. Just as in Russia, where during the period of Bolshevism Tartarized sub-humans murdered anyone who by his tall form and confident gait could be suspected of

[10] Admiral Gaspard de Coligny (1519–72). Rosenberg is merely pointing to figures whom he considers representative of Nordic influence in French history. (Ed.)

being a master, so also did that black, Jacobin rabble drag
to the scaffold anybody who was lean and blond. To put
it in terms of racial history: if the Nordic racial strengths
in France were not completely broken by the fall of the
Huguenots, they were at least strongly suppressed. Classical France displayed only intellect without nobility, a
character defect which was instinctively seized upon by
hungry people, who were acting in common with other
grasping sub-humans, to dispose of the last clear heads of
France. Since that time, the Mediterranean-Alpine Man
mixed type (not the 'Celtic' type) has stepped into the
foreground. Shopkeepers, lawyers and speculators have
become the masters of public life. Democracy—i.e. not
the rule of character, but that of money—had begun.
It didn't matter whether France was monarchical or
republican, because nineteenth-century man remained
racially uncreative. However, because of this, Jewish
bankers also pushed themselves into the foreground,
followed by Jewish journalists and Marxists. French
power-politics remained constant only because of the
traditions of a thousand-year history combined with
similar geographical influences. But this was manifested
in a fashion different from that which had appeared
between the fourteenth and sixteenth centuries. Those in
France who still thought nobly drew back from the dirty
business of politics, lived in provincial castles in conservative isolation, and sent their sons into the army to serve
only the fatherland. This was particularly so in the case
of the navy. At the end of the nineteenth century, on-
lookers at naval balls made the astonishing discovery that
all the officers were blond!*

This strength, which still existed in northern France

* Stackelberg, *Ein Leben im baltischen Kampfe* (München, 1927).

(Normandy, during the period of heresies, was always considered as 'little Germany'), stood in opposition to the German Reich in 1914. However, this strength was no longer directed by blood-relations but by the bankers Rothschild and by other financial powers bound to them by race. Included among this type would be people like Fallières, Millerand or many of the Marxist leaders, characterized by an Alpine impotence. So even today we can observe the trickling away of the last worthwhile blood. Entire stretches of land in the south of Europe have already dried out and these regions are now sucking in Africans, just as Rome itself had once done. Toulon and Marseilles are continuously transmitting new germs of bastardization into the countryside. An ever more degenerate population streams about the Notre Dame in Paris. Negroes and mulattoes stroll about on the arms of white women; a purely Jewish quarter, with new synagogues, arises. Disgusting mestizo snobs pollute that race of still beautiful women, which is being enticed away from the rest of France to Paris. Thus we are now experiencing an event which has already been played out in Athens, Rome and Persepolis. This is why a close alliance with France—completely apart from political and military issues—would be so dangerous. On the contrary, the task of today means: defence against the infiltrating hordes of Africa; closing frontiers on the basis of anthropological characteristics; and the establishment of a Nordic-European coalition in order to cleanse the European motherland of the ever-expanding disease-centres of Africa and Syria. Even for the benefit of the French themselves ...

*　　*　　*

Such a task is endowed with increasing urgency due to the degeneracy that has befallen Europe since 1918. Rosenberg also attacks those who seek to defend German security through some form of alliance with Russia.

The nation's blood-sacrifices upon all the battlefields of the world gave the democratic men of the East and their bastardized assistants of the metropolis an opportunity for revival. That human type which, 150 years ago, had begun to appear as openly dominant in France, also appeared in Germany after 1918, financed with the gold of Syria and at the head of democracy. This type knew nothing of the older values, but fought against them, openly and with great insolence, on all the streets and squares ('The stupidest ideal is the ideal of heroism,' said the *Berliner Tageblatt*). Lucky speculators were transformed into men of honour. Eastern-Jewish bankers became financiers for the 'state-preserving' parties, but those who fought against this mockery of the German essence were tossed into prison on grounds of 'lese-majesty'. This transmutation of values is accompanied by transmutation in the ruling blood, and even a single glance at the line-up of Marxist-democratic leaders attests in fearful fashion to racial decline—something that can be observed if one compares the majestic heads of Moltke, Bismarck, Roon and Wilhelm I with those of the parliamentarians who, until 1933, governed the Börse-colony of Germany.

In this hour of fearful despair on the part of the worthy *Volk*-element, domination of this freshly-scrubbed Alpine-Jewish strata seemed assured through its immediate, self-interested alliance with strong forces in contemporary France; a France whose worn-out ideas they used to supplement the spiritual poverty of the 1918 revolt. Through their lies they had become great and could no longer deviate from their course. Therefore, German democracy, a form of French politics, in the *final analysis* can be traced back to the 'natural' sympathies of these men of decline, who feeling their delineated character to be a living reproach, thus attempt to ally themselves to anything that is as decayed as they are. This also explains the sympathies which post-revolutionary Russia calls forth in all centres of Marxist sub-humanity. Behind all the glitter of pallid 'real-political' considerations and so on, is gathered a stream of sub-conscious racial strengths, strengths that are linked to a stagnant flood of the refuse of race-chaos. It runs counter to historical tradition and territorial-political legitimacy and hence is harmful to the German nation.

*   *   *

Thus we can see that Rosenberg deified history, albeit a grossly distorted history, for the purpose of glorifying the Aryan race; a race which once had been Europe-wide but was now mainly, although not exclusively, concentrated in Germany. Rosenberg was perfectly consistent in describing what he felt to be the salient characteristics of this race.

Today, a new belief is arising: the *Mythus* of the blood; the belief that the godly essence of man itself is to be defended through the blood; that belief which embodies the clearest knowledge that the Nordic race represents that *Mysterium* which has overthrown and replaced the old sacraments.

Spanning history from the present, the many-faceted

character of Nordic creative strength lies stretched out
before us. Aryan India bequeathed to the world a meta-
physic whose depths have yet to be plumbed, even today.
The Aryan Persian composed for us the *religious* myths
from which we still draw sustenance. Doric Hellas
dreamed of a *beauty*, which, as we see it in completed form
before us, will never be further developed. Italian Rome
illustrates for us an example of formal *state loyalty*; how a
threatened human community must organize and defend
itself. And German Europe bequeathed to the world the
radiant ideal of humanity, as exemplified in its teaching
that *character value* must be the foundation of all morality,
and in its paean to the highest value of the Nordic being —
to the idea of freedom of conscience and of *honour*. All
military and scholarly struggles revolve around this ideal
and if, in the great struggle to come, this idea is not
victorious, all the West and its blood will perish, as India
and Hellas once did, vanishing into eternity in chaos.

In recognizing that Europe and all its creative products
result from character, we have uncovered the underlying
theme of European religion, German scholarship and even
Nordic art. To become inwardly conscious of this fact, to
experience it with the full beat of an heroic heart, is to
prepare the way for rebirth. This recognition is the
foundation for a new *Weltanschauung*, a new-yet-old theory
of state, the *Mythus* of that new life-feeling which, alone,
will give us the strength to overthrow the presumptuous
domination of sub-humans and to create a unique
civilization which will penetrate into all areas of life.

... Each race has its soul, each soul its race — its own
unique inner and outer architectonic shape, its characteristic form of appearance and characteristic expression of
life style, and unique relationships between the strengths

of will and reason. Each race cultivates, as its fixed goal, only *one* high ideal. If this should be transformed or overthrown by another system of allegiance or by an overpowering intrusion of foreign blood and foreign ideas, the external consequence of this inner metamorphosis is chaos, designated as epochs of catastrophe ...

It is possible that, after such catastrophes, the strengths of soul group themselves anew around the old focal points, and under new conditions even give birth to a new form of being. This could result either from a final victory over foreign values, whose intrusion was merely temporary, or from the gradual crystallization of a second focal point. However, if two or more *Weltanschauungen*, derived from different highest values, occupy a common place in time or space, and each *Weltanschauung* is meant to be shared by a *common* group of people, this signifies the existence of an unhealthy palliative which bears within itself the germs of a new collapse. If a penetrating system succeeds in weakening belief in old ideas and in decomposing or subjugating — even physically — the races and peoples who bear these ideas, then this signifies the death of a culture-soul which then disappears, in its outward manifestations, from the earth.

The life of a race does not represent a logically-developed philosophy nor even the unfolding of a pattern according to natural law, but rather the development of a mystical synthesis, an activity of soul, which cannot be explained rationally, nor can it be conceived through a study of cause and effect. Interpretation of the culture-core necessitates an exposure of the religious, moral, philosophical, scientific or aesthetic values which determine the total rhythm of the culture, and which also determine the relationships and classification of human resources. A *Volk* that is primarily religiously-orientated will produce a culture different from one which prescribes as its form of being perception, or beauty. *In the final analysis, any philosophy which goes beyond a formal critique of reason is less a mode of perception than one of faith*; a psychic and racial faith, a faith in character values.

Our contemporary age of chaos had been conjured up centuries ago. Owing to certain circumstances, the life-laws of Nordic-conditioned peoples have been weakened through the intervention of other strengths; in many places these have supplanted belief in our own posited highest values, or they have succeeded in placing these values in a subordinate role in a new system. The race-soul of Northern Europe stands in persistent conflict with these phenomena of decadence, despite the constant emergence of new centres of enemy strength.

The nineteenth century revealed the existence of three fully developed and contiguous systems. The first one was that of the Nordic West, the system which was originally based upon freedom of the soul and the idea of honour; the second was the complete system of Roman dogma, which required a humble, submissive love in the service of a unified-governed priesthood; the third was the open harbinger of chaos—the system of limitless, materialistic individualism, with its final goal being the establishment of money as the unifying, type-building strength in the political-economic world.

These three powers were continuously displacing themselves and battling for the soul of every European. Even in the last century, men were summoned to fight and to die in the names of freedom, honour and *Volkstum*. However, 1918 brought victory to the powers of pluto-cracy and the Roman Church. Even in the midst of a most fearsome collapse, though, the old Nordic race-soul was aroused to a newer and higher level of consciousness. It fully understood that the coexistence of different, necessarily self-contained, value systems on an equal basis was impossible and that what it—in its customary generosity—thought to be right (toleration of other value systems), had in fact led to its present degeneration. It understood that it could incorporate elements which were racially and spiritually related; but that foreign elements would have to be ruthlessly cut off, or beaten down if necessary, not because they were in themselves 'false' or 'bad', but because they were *alien* and destructive of the inner core of our being. Today, we feel it to be our duty to be able, with the utmost clarity, to hold ourselves to account—either to acknowledge the highest values and enduring ideas of the German West, or to destroy ourselves, body and soul. For ever. The *real* struggle today therefore, does not so much involve, as it did earlier, meeting external power displacements with inner compromise, but the reverse: it is the struggle to revitalize the spiritual cells of Nordic-conditioned peoples, it concerns the reinstatement to ruling authority of those ideas and values from which everything that signifies culture for us stems. It concerns the preservation of the racial substance itself. Perhaps, for a time, the distribution of power will continue to be unpropitious for us. However, if we can anywhere ever experience and create a new-yet-old type of German who, conscious of soul, race and history, unflinchingly proclaims and embodies the old-yet-new values, all who stumble in darkness and yet are rooted in the old homeland soil of Europe will rally around this core.

* * *

A racially-conscious Volk, *i.e. one that has grasped the harsh laws of nature, must eschew traditional forms of individualistic or universalistic humanitarian thinking; likewise, it must understand that 'freedom' itself is a term that must be grasped in its* Volkish *context. To be racially-conscious means to have grasped the mystery of blood.*

The search after an 'absolute truth' has been paralleled by a phenomenon not confined to today—the wholly different conception of I and thou, of I and the world, of I and eternity; the so-called organic approach. Leibniz was opposed to the mechanical atomism of someone like Hobbes, who maintained that society, a totality, originated from an adding together of unformed pieces. In opposition to the absolutist doctrine which stated that there were given abstract eternal laws of form which had to be filled out by individuals, Leibniz claimed that the blending together of the individual and the general consummated itself in the form of individuality and, in so doing, this synthesis concretizes itself in a living, unique manner. A mathematical schematicism, which posited a logically-comprehensible *immutable* Being, would inhibit the perception of the *Becoming* of self-forming Being: the value of this Becoming lies precisely in consciousness of possible perfection through *self*-development. In one forward-striving advance towards self, the solutions necessitated by atomism, mechanicism, individualism and universalism, solutions to pedantically posited problems of existence, were transformed and nullified. Through this, however, a new morality was established: the soul does not adhere to abstract rules imposed from the outside; neither does it move towards a goal posited from without; in no case does it go outside itself, but rather, comes to itself.

With this, however, a rather different conception of truth is outlined: for us, truth does not mean that which is *logical* and that which is false; rather, it demands an *organic* answer to the question: fruitful or unfruitful; self-governed or unfree.

Similarly, Herder, who in *one* way was seeking a 'humanistic' absolute, penetrated even more deeply into the great thought of Leibniz and became a teacher specially ordained for our time, as have very few, even among the greatest. With Leibniz, soul and totality still stood apart from one another, as two completely representative Beings; the 'windowless' monads could be posited as being linked to each other only through accepting the proposition that, even in this condition, the uniform purification process of self-development completes itself, i.e. the monads themselves 'reflect' it. Herder posited 'national consciousness' as constituting the life-endowed link between the two entities. Life became endowed with its own unique value, apart from all rational law. Just as each man and *Volk* stand as living and unique entities, so also does each of them embody and retain unique value, i.e. a phenomenon of a moral nature which does not drown in the stream of any given chain of 'progress', but which maintains itself as an entity, and justly so. This growth (organic) phenomenon is conditioned by inner values; however, it is also defined through limitation—if one has to use this word. The phenomenon must either be rejected or confirmed totally. The forced introduction of abstraction would annihilate the form as a whole, as well as its potential. Herder consciously heaped scorn upon the pretentious savants of 'progress' who sought to measure the forms of life by the infantile scale of the Enlightenment. He then uttered a phrase which is relevant to our own age and our joyful message: *'Each nation has its centre of happiness within itself as each sphere has its own centre of gravity.'** Many people rallied around this mysterious 'centre'. The Romantics had already designated *Volksgeist* as the most essential element of our life. Schleiermacher taught that 'each man has to represent humanity in his *own* manner so that in the fullness of eternity everything that can come out of its womb' will be realized. Nietzsche, with all that unique passion and out of rebellion against narrow schematicism, later demanded a higher life and sought out the truth in the individual personality. Only what life creates has virtue. Life says, 'Do not seek me, but thyself.' Ranke,† in the middle of his factual representations says that if Europe (after Rome) again allowed itself to be dominated by an international principle, an organic-national movement would rise up against it with primitive strength. Elsewhere Ranke, almost paradoxically,‡ proclaimed that 'Each epoch is immediate to God, and its value subsists not in what results from it, but in its *own existence*, in its own self.'

As opposed to the scholastic-logical-mechanical struggle towards 'Absolute Knowledge', this is the other, the 'truer' stream of veritable growth (organic) — searching for truth. For the most complete unfolding of self stems from experiencing 'the centre of happiness', and in the language of this book this means: *from the experienced Mythus of the Nordic racial soul serve the honour of the Volk in love.*

Is the soul made in the image of God and immortal?

* Herder, *Auch eine Philosophie der Geschichte der Menscheit.*
† Ranke, *Geschichte der Päpste.*
‡ Ranke, *Über die Epochen der neueren Geschichte,* 1 Vortrag.

On questions like this, the searcher for truth who uses only logic will carefully weigh up every possible reason, for or against. He will then either give up altogether, or provide 'proof' for his yes-or-no answer. The growth-conscious searcher for truth, however, will *maintain* and *avow* the yes or no. The belief in the intrinsic value of personality, the monad, in its God-like nature and immortality, is an exemplary landmark of the Christian and also the non-Christian Nordic-German thinker. This belief, although it assumed different forms in different historical epochs, has been brought to fruition by great artists, heroes and statesmen, but *it* has in turn sustained them. And this fruitfulness points to a truth which is more valuable to us than those possible conclusions, based on analogy, which we could obtain on that way which seeks goals in an organic manner; to wit, there arises in the moral-metaphysical field something which we had also recognized in the field of art: that true form and its contents as they appear in a given phenomenon are not to be separated from one another; that with the surrender of a form which corresponds to our own measure to the form of a fictitious abstract, eternal, absolute truth, we not only do *not* come any nearer to the 'truth', but actually push further away any possibility of approaching it. It also becomes self-evident here that art will live among us again only if our Being partakes of true life. Our *Katheder* philosophers visualize 'absolute truth' in 'the union of the finite with the infinite', whereupon the '*Volkish* truth' would have to be submitted to the test of whether it represented, in this sense, a closer approximation to the 'one truth'. In this, however, it has been forgotten that we, *above all* lack *any* form of standard to make such a judgment; for in order to be able effectively to reach a decision, each of us would have to be in full possession of the accepted 'eternal, one truth'. In this case, therefore, it would be well to focus upon a completely different centre than that of logical-rational calculation of truth; perhaps even upon that 'centre of happiness' which Herder suggested and which suggests that we could become 'one with ourselves', a state which was once longed for by Meister Eckhart. It would be well worth it if the *predominance* of scholastic-humanistic-classical schematicism were stripped away in favour of the organic-racial-*Volkish Weltanschauung*. Naturally, critical points of view should not be deprecated at this point.

From the insight that reason-determined, definable experience of the formal variety does not determine life, but rather simply represents or can represent a heuristic principle, there arise two new attitudes to the belief in the Aryan. One attitude desires that fading beliefs be revived again, while the other shuns this undertaking and, hinting at its specious longing, declares that so little is known about it that nothing more can be established on the subject. Both parties are wrong, because they have falsely formulated the question. The question does not involve acknowledging the validity of the form of belief, but rather perception of soul and character values. Time-conditioned experiential forms are combined with their special life-feelings; the race-soul seizes upon old questions in newer forms; *however, the constructive strengths of will and soul remain, in direction and nature, the same.* Here alone, however, one can grasp the essence and history of Nordic man, at least after the deceased centre is experienced anew. Thus, the 'noble' soul, inner freedom and honour remain, and serve to condition everything else—

but only as long as related blood flows through the veins of the millions of Northern Europe. Thus, 'eternal truth' means all-around veracity.

We have come to an end. The Leibnizian monad stands 'windowless' *vis-à-vis* its counterpart and both are equally rich personalities. Herder and his followers already were seeking the mediation of *Volk*. Today we can add the following to previous consideration ... If confronted with a personality of a totally foreign face the monad becomes 'windowless' again; solitude will lead to withdrawal. No bridge of true understanding can link it to a Chinese, much less to the essence of a Syrian or African bastard. Thus the entities in which existence is realized are not monads and 'humanity'; rather, these are personality and race.

Through this insight we are able to draw into the light of complete consciousness another illness of our day: this is universal relativity. Individualism is recognized as being just as 'relative' as undifferentiated universalism. Both strive continuously to attain an understandable logic and, because of these efforts, both are shattered. When this happens, the organic, *Volkish Weltanschauung* comes into its own, as it has always led the way whenever mechanical individualism and schematic universalism have sought to put the world in chains. The philosophical systematizers instinctively draw back from this testament to Nordic Being, because the essence of this wilful impulse represents no logical system, but signifies rather an inundation of soul. Today, in the midst of a collapsing atomistic epoch, this true, organic *Weltanschauung* demands its right, its fundamental right, to an ever greater degree. This *Weltanschauung* stemming from honour, which is in turn the highest value of the Nordic-Western world, should be allowed to partake of its core with lofty bliss and be able to reformulate life anew, without fear.

The individualistic dogma whereby each individual being exists *for itself*, and 'humanity' consists of all the individual peoples added together, this dogma today has been finally excluded from serious consideration. The most significant observation ... that universalism is the twin-brother of individualism is justified, in that this universalism suffers from the same defect as its ostensible opponent. Both are intellectualistic, i.e. opposed to nature. The universalist school (O. Spann),[11] successfully contradicted the materialistic and stupid individualism, only to fall into the same error out of which the latter school was born. In pure abstraction, a gradation of the spiritual has been erected; a new schematic, constructivistic conception of the world has been introduced. On the basis of the old Platonic myth that species comes before type, the following 'intellectual gradation of historical human societies' was introduced: humanity, culture-group, *Volk*-group, nationality, tribe-affiliation, native homeland *Volk*-membership. It is being emphasized through this classification that humanity comes before culture-group, culture-group comes before *Volk*-group, etc. Even today, some are attempting to make this rather suspect ladder of materials and values more palatable by claiming that a totally symmetrical separation of organically united parts does not necessarily follow from this spiritual ranking. This is most clearly revealed with

[11] An example of Rosenberg's bitterness towards intellectual opposition, even from those close to him—Othmar Spann, a believer in *Gemeinschaft* sociology and in the corporate state, once addressed Rosenberg's Combat League for German Culture (in 1929). In some respects Spann's notions on state and society were similar to Rosenberg's, but Spann's corporatism was derived from his Catholicism. Rosenberg never really forgave him for this. (Ed.)

regard to nationality (*Volkstum*), while culture-group and humanity appear to be more faded and less easy to grasp. We can already see here the great break in the universalistic method of research: on the one hand it holds firm to a purely intellectualistic system of classification and pursues a neo-scholastic course; on the other hand, through compliments, it has to add on a more organic research method, which adheres to life-laws, as a related approach. With admittedly desirable clarity the following is established: 'A super-political church is more important than the *Volkish* church;' and after an exposition stating that religion is established before the state: 'From this, it of course follows that the state, as the highest institution rules over the specialized institution of the church; that, however, the state obtains its spiritual rationale from religion to the same degree as the church itself, and thus from *a religion which has been organized and formed by the church, for there is no other kind.*'* Here, the universalist school is unmasked. We can see that it obtains its name not on the basis of pure factual-philosophical grounds, but that it emerges from theocratic conviction. Now, we can understand further what is truly meant by the concept 'separation of organically united parts': in the final analysis it means the gushing out of the contents contained in 'humanity' or in 'organized religion'; for from where else could this separation originate if nationality is a third-rate power without *organic* ancestry?

If Oswald Spengler wanted to construct a history of form whose primary data consisted of heaven-sent 'culture-groups', Othmar Spann, as a modern spokesman for medieval scholasticism, watered this down yet further

* O. Spann, *Gesellschaftsphilosophie* (München, 1928), pp. 103, 107, 109, and so on.

through his ostensibly superior posture of a thinker who organizes everything 'from above'. *Here* our heuristic principle — even though it is completely contained in the intellectual scheme which puts race before variety — comes into its own; as a method which seeks out *growth* from below, it constitutes an organic resistance to these methods of pure intellectualism. We posit the following divisions, which adhere to the laws of life: 1. Race-soul; 2. Nationality; 3. Personality; 4. Culture-circle. By this we do not mean to suggest a table of ranks going from top to bottom, but a continuously pulsating circulation. The race-soul cannot be felt with one's hand, and yet it is represented in nationality which is tied together by blood, and it [the race-soul] is both crowned by and reflected in the great personalities who, working creatively, nurture a culture-group, which again will be borne by race and race-soul. This totality is not only 'spirit', but 'spirit' and will, therefore a totality of life. In such a fashion that 'separation of organically-united parts', as embodied in nationality, leads back organically to its blood-soulish *primary* source, not to essenceless culture-groups and bloodless combinations of humanity, about which we have no evidence. For this reason a truly accomplished and rich *Volkskultur* can develop, almost of necessity, from our scheme.

With the above insight the organic philosophy of our time has disposed of the tyranny of intellectual schemes, of that purely schematic and intellectual process which manufactures matrices in the belief that it can encapsulate races and peoples; the sub-conscious or conscious intention of this being to use them as means towards some kind of 'final unity'. When Spann, in opposition to the wisdom of rhe Ancient Greeks, maintains that *God* is the measure

of all things, but that religion can be found only in the
[Catholic] Church, since there is 'no other', this viewpoint is unmasked as one which maintains that the *priest*
is the measure of all things. Opposed to this the newly-
born *Weltanschauung* of our time declares that the race-
bound *Volk*-soul is the measure of all our thought, longing
of will and activities; it is the last measure of our value.
Materialistic individualism as well as anti-natural
universalism in all its roles—from Roman theocracy to
the humanitarianism of freemasonry—are fallen for all
time. However, the whole 'general' aesthetic of the
last two centuries is also fallen. The entire, bloodless,
internationalistic rubbish-heap which, like the Spanish
Boot,[12] had tormented and would have continued to
torment us, has been blown away. A singular but decisive
transformation of our spiritual position has been completed, and without the bitter tumult which this has
caused for other races. A new centre of our Being—spark-
ling, glorious and life-filled—has come into joyful activity.
This new-and-yet-old blood *Mythus*, the numerous
falsifications of which have been elaborated, was threatened from within our own nation, when dark satanic
strengths became active behind the victorious armies of
1914; when once again there dawned an age when the
Fenris Wolf broke his chains, when Hel,[13] exuding the
odour of decay, moved over the earth and the *Midgard-
schlange* stirred the oceans of the world. Millions upon
millions were ready to sacrifice themselves to attain but
one result embodied in the phrase: for the honour and
freedom of the *Volk*. The world inferno continued to the
end; nonetheless, sacrifices were demanded and made by

[12] Sixteenth-century instrument of torture. (Ed.)
[13] Nordic goddess of the underworld and of the dead. (Ed.)

all. All that was revealed, however, was that behind the armies daemonic powers had triumphed over divine ones. Unrestrained, they raged unbound throughout the world, stirring up new unrest, new flames, new destruction. However, at the same time that *Mythus* of the blood, for which heroes had died, stirred anew in the bowed souls of those left behind by the departed warriors, until this *Mythus* was grasped and experienced in its final ramifications. The inner voice now demands that the myth of blood and the myth of soul, race and ego, *Volk* and personality, blood and honour; that this myth, alone and uncomprisingly, must penetrate, bear and determine all life. It demands that, for the German people, the two million dead heroes must not have died in vain. It demands a world revolution and will tolerate no high values in its vicinity other than its own. Personalities must rally around the centre of the *Volk* and race-soul, around that mysterious centre which makes fruitful the very cadence of German Being and Becoming whenever Germany draws close to it. It is that nobility, that freedom of the mystical soul, conscious of honour, which once in an outpouring never since equalled streamed over Germany's borders to self-sacrifice. The individual soul died for the freedom and honour to elevate itself; for its own *Volkstum*. Alone, *this* sacrifice can determine the coming life-rhythm of the German people, it alone, in the hard conscious discipline obtained through that which he has learned and experienced can nurture the new type of German.

This old-yet-new *Mythus* already has activated and embraced millions of souls. With a thousand tongues it cries out today that we did not 'run our course around 1800', but that, for the first time, and with heightened consciousness and flowing will, we want to become a total

Volk, 'at one with ourselves', something Meister Eckhart once longed for. For hundreds of thousands of souls *Mythus* is not something that can be relegated with pedantic superiority to being an intellectual curio, but is rather the cellular rebirth of the spiritual centre. The credo of the new age is 'Alone, I will'—the attitude of Faust as he pressed forward through all fields of knowledge. It is the credo of an age which calls for a new future, and this *will* is our fate. However, this will does not merely 'recognize' the essence of old and new cultures in order to draw itself around them; rather, in self-conscious recognition of the highest values bequeathed to us by our own culture-group, it shuns them as limiting. That our researchers remain transfixed by historical forms without being able to construct anything themselves only demonstrates that their will to construct has been broken. There is no justification, however, in saying that their own unproductivity is the fate of the whole. The new *Mythus* and the new type-creating strength which today is struggling within us for expression cannot be 'confronted'. It, itself, will break its own trail and *create* facts.

*   *   *

Quite naturally a Volk *that has grasped the* Mythus *of blood must realize that the term 'freedom' can be apprehended only in its* Volkish *context. Hence there is a peculiar yet heroic freedom which is specifically Aryan.*

...Freedom, in the German sense, consists of an inner independence, the possibility to explore, to create a world view—it is a true, religious feeling. For the Near-Eastern dispersions and their kin, freedom means the unrestrained annihilation of other cultural values. The first was once embodied in the high cultural development of Greece. However, after even the Near-Eastern slaves were 'recognized as men', this creation was completely destroyed. Today, everybody indiscriminately speaks of an external 'freedom', one which can only deliver us to race chaos. Freedom means fellowship of race. Only this can guarantee the highest possible development. Racial fellowship, however, necessitates *protection* of the race.

II. NORDIC RELIGION

Throughout even his more specialized writings on race and race history, Rosenberg made specific references to religion. As we have seen, he indicated that there are 'positive' and 'negative' varieties of Christianity. The latter he identified with the emerging Catholic Church, particularly as it was influenced by that Jewish preacher of race-chaos, St Paul. The former was an Aryan creation. Rosenberg summarized the differences between the two strands by polarizing them under the all-inclusive rubrics love and honour.

The Volk-religion *of Rosenberg—the emphasis upon honour and denigration of love and the* Volkish *embodiment of God—found roots in the writings of Meister Eckhart (1260–1327?), an individual to whom Rosenberg's speculations would no doubt have seemed rather strange. However, Rosenberg's 'religion' had antecedents in German cultural history, as did so much of the Nazi ideology. His rejection of the Old Testament and his attacks upon St Paul, as well as his denial of creation, can all be found in the writings of Johann Gottlieb Fichte (1762–1814), who was also a racist. Paul de Lagarde (1827–91) was another contributor to the Rosenberg idea of* Volk-religion, *a doctrine which called to life the teachings of a not insignificant mystic and elevated them in the name of an anti-Christian* Mythus. *Odin had* not *died; rather, he had been armed with an eschatological zeal that transcended Valhalla. This chapter consists of extracts from* Der Mythus des 20. Jahrhunderts.

There are two values which embody the almost two-thousand-year-old conflict between church and race, theology and belief, enforced belief and pride in character; two values which are rooted in will and which are now battling for supremacy in Europe: love and honour. Each is striving for recognition as the *highest* value. The Church, strange as this might sound, wants to *rule* through love; Nordic Europeans want to freely live and die in honour. Both ideas have found their respective martyrs, yet, as obvious as this is, the conflict often has not been seen with clarity.

This insight has been reserved for our own time. It is a mythical occurrence, and yet is as clear as sunlight.

Love and pity, honour and duty are spiritual essences which, stripped of their various external coverings, represent the driving strengths within the lives of almost all races and nations capable of culture. Accordingly, first the love concept in its most common form, and then the honour concept attained primacy in direct relationship to the *Weltanschauungen* and general characteristics of the respective peoples; characteristics which were reflected in the goals for which they strived. One or the other ideal constituted the standard against which all thinking and activity was measured. However, one or the other ideal must *predominate* in order to be able to create the *determining* characteristics for a given period. Nowhere is the struggle between these two ideals more tragically evident than in the conflicts between the Nordic races (including its various peoples) and their contemporary racial and ideological surroundings.

In confronting the rising question of which motif, above all others, has proved itself to be the decisive one as far as the state- and culture-building capacities of the Nordic race are concerned, we must answer that it is the concept of honour and, bound up inseparably with this, the concept of duty which arises out of consciousness of inner freedom. The moment, however, in which love and pity (or, if one wants, compassion) become predominant, racial-*Volkish* and cultural degeneration begin to occur in all Nordic-conditioned states.

... If the concept of honour has been anywhere the centre of Being, it has attained this level in the Nordic, German West. The Viking appeared on the historical scene with an historically unique self-assurance. An uninhibited feeling of freedom nurtured that population expansion which propelled one Nordic wave after another over the nations of the world. With lavish expenditures of blood and heroic imperturbability, the Vikings established states in Russia, Sicily, England and France. Here, there ruled rough-hewn racial tribes, without obligation or breeding, uninhibited by cultivated reflection upon purpose or upon a previously-determined legal order. The only serious concern that characterized the Norsemen was the concept of personal honour. It was honour and freedom which drove these individuals towards distant realms and towards independence— towards regions in which there was land to master; or, to the last man, they abandoned their courts and castles to fight for liberty. This ingenuous lack of purpose, far removed from considerations of trade, was the principle of Nordic man, when, despite his wild, youthful enthusiasm, he took a constructive part in the history of the West. At first, a small group of followers would gather around inspired leaders, and gradually this led to the erection of certain social ethics; finally, after the foray, a rustic settling process followed (those in the South, of course, decayed quickly, disintegrating rapidly in the face of late-Oriental opulence).

For the historical observer, there hardly appears another instance in which the position of a people was so purely and completely shaped by its own intrinsic values. All power and possessions, every obligation, every activity stood in the service of honour and, when necessary, life was sacrificed in its name—without qualms or whimpering. The law of honour ruled over life to the same degree as it was reflected in poetry; it was the cornerstone of the saga-world and no word is encountered as often as the word honour. This, the Nordic hero-world, even with all the wild confusion which stemmed from an over-abundance of subjectivism, constituted a unity in essence and in development.*

It augurs well that such an insight can be found among German teaching circles, a group that up till now has been deluded by pseudo-classical aestheticism. *Here* we have touched upon the central nerve of our entire history; our whole future as Germans, as Europeans, will be decided by the degree to which we value the honour concept. Even if the Old-Nordic man from time to time acted irrationally, the honour-conscious core of his Being evinced, even in struggle and death, an air of purity. War could be conducted brutally, but it was considered the foremost duty of Nordic man that he admit to his kills. (Krieck.) This feeling of responsibility that was demanded of each and every personality constituted

* Krieck, *Menschenformung*, p. 154.

the most effective defence against moral stagnation, against the hypocritical disintegration of values which, in the course of Western history, has appeared in the several forms of humaneness that have come over us like an insidious temptation. Sometimes, this has called itself democracy, sometimes social compassion, sometimes humility and love. The personal honour of the Norseman demanded courage and self-discipline. Unlike the Greek heroes, he did not sweat for hours before every battle; unlike the Greek, he did not cry out if he was wounded— on the contrary, his honour demanded that he compose himself and muster his strength. Seen from this *point of view*, the Viking is really the *Kulturmensch*, while the aesthetically washed-out later Greek was the backward, soft-centred barbarian. The saying of Fichte, 'True culture is *character culture*' [*Gesinnungskultur*] reveals our true Nordic essence even as it stands in contrast to other cultures whose highest values are not those of character— which for us is synonymous with honour and duty—but cultures which encompass their lives with another senti- ment, another idea.

The fortunes of the Western peoples have been varied, as they have been shaped by different conditions in the course of time. Generally, where Nordic blood pre- dominates, the honour concept has remained the primary one. However, this is so even when mixed with other ideals ... In Russia, the idea of religiosity, of a religious feeling, has been predominant to such an extent that even the wildest outburst is often masked by a shell of religious fervour (for example, in Dostoevsky's *The Idiot*, there is the man who, before murdering somebody to obtain his silver watch, mutters a prayer); thus the Russian refers to his fatherland as ... 'Holy Russia'. The Frenchman approaches life from a formal-aesthetic point of view; therefore, for him, France is 'La Belle France'. The same is true of the Italian. The Englishman is proud of his consistent historical development, of tradition and of stolid, unchanging customs. Therefore, he admires his 'Old England'. In spite of there being many unhallowed qualities among us, we continue to speak with constant fervour of 'German sincerity' [*Deutsche Treue*], which proves that our metaphysical Being continually seeks out the 'mark of honour' as its point of reference.

The continuous struggle, which had already raged for a millennium, centred around this human concept; this occurred when Northern Europe saw itself in opposition to the armed Roman South which, in the name of religion and Christian love, finally subjugated it. Beyond question, an epoch of German history—the age of myths—would have come to an end even without the attack of armed Roman-Syrian Christianity.

Nature symbolism would have yielded to a new moral-metaphysical system, a new form of belief. However, this form would no doubt have consisted of the same spiritual values and would have had the idea of honour as its leitmotif and standard. Now, another spiritual value swept through Christendom and assumed first place: love—in the sense of humility, compassion, submissiveness and asceticism. Today, it has become clear to every upright German that with the doctrine of love, one which embraces in equal measure all the creatures of the world, a sensitive blow had been struck against the soul of Northern Europe. Christianity, as it has built itself up as a system, knew nothing of racial-*Volkish* thinking, because it represented a massive blending together of different elements. *Moreover, it knew nothing of the idea of honour,* *either, because in pursuance of its late-Roman period power goals, it subjugated not only bodies, but souls also.* It is noteworthy, however, that the thought of love was never able to penetrate the *leadership* of the Church establishment. The expansion of the Roman system, from the first day on has been characterized by dogmatically principled and consciously intolerant organization, one which has taken a negative, if not hostile, attitude towards all other systems. Where it could, it proceeded with excommunication, ostracism, fire, sword and poison in order to assure its own existence. Moral considerations aside, we can be sure of these facts, ones which have not been denied ever by modern Roman Catholic publicists. More than anything else, these facts prove that the 'love' idea contains no type-building strength, *for even the organization of the 'religion of love' has been built without it,* and in an even more unloving way than other type-creating powers. As Döllinger testified—the old gods tolerated Catholic as well as other beliefs and demonstrated respect for them as spiritual needs for belief. All of this disappeared whenever the spirit of 'Boniface' and the compulsory rule of 'love' triumphed.* It was not easy for any German to be outspoken in expressing any negative evaluation of the Etruscan-Jewish-Roman system for, no matter how the system had spread, *it has become*

---

* Compare, for example, in contrast to the Roman will to persecute, the position of the 'heathen' Frisian Duke Radbod. He remained true to the belief of his fathers; however, he did persecute Christian preachers. When once several especially diligent Christian apostles were brought before him, and in the face of great abuse one of them continued to stand up for the new faith with great bravery, the heathen Duke said: 'I see that thou dost not fear our threats, and that thy words are as thy work.' He then sent the preacher back 'with all honours to Pippin, Duke of the Franks'. Thus it is reported by Alcuin. In so far as nobility of soul is concerned, this heathen Frisian Prince stands far above the 'representatives of God' in Rome, who have set out to purge the world of this inner freedom and respect.

ennobled through the devotion of millions of Germans. It assimilated both foreign and spiritually-related attractions,
paying little heed to the first, and hoping to shape the
second in terms of prevailing Nordic values. Nevertheless,
today, in an age of great spiritual upheaval, honesty
requires that we examine the positive and negative aspects
of Rome, using as a criterion its effect upon the innate
essence of the German West. This is not done out of
personal feelings of ill will, but in order to gain a comprehensive view of the tremendous tensions and explosions
that have occurred within its [the Church's] two-thou-
sand-year history, and to investigate the racial-spiritual
values that conditioned these upheavals. Thus we can see
that essentially the same struggles as beset the Greeks and
Romans befell the Germans. The Germans could just as
little escape this struggle as the two other great Nordic
peoples, because as the latter receded they bore within
themselves both Asiatic spiritual values and the human
material in which these values were embodied, phenomena which they had once suppressed. They bore these
Asian values to Hellas, over the Alps, over the borders of
the Germanic territories, and after a while, into the
heart of the Nordic race itself.

If, however, one searches for the source of this great
success, one will discover that—besides the early technical
superiority of the older, more experienced South and the
period of religious crisis in German life, factors which
would not explain so long-lasting a victory—one of the
most important contributions was the appeal to German
generosity; that naivety as exemplified in Siegfried, which
presupposes that even one's opponent has the same
honour values and open form of combat; that childlike
inability to recognize, even with time, the opposite.

These qualities have led to many great defeats in the course of German history: at the time when Germans were beginning to admire Rome and in recent times when Jewish emancipation was pushed through and was allowed the poison of equality to mix with healthy blood. The first blunder exacted a fearful retribution in the wars against heretics and in the Thirty Years War, which brought Germany to the edge of the abyss; the second is exacting the same retribution today, as the poisoned body of the German *Volk* lies in convulsions. And *again* and *again* both of these enemy powers call upon the generosity of the heavily afflicted, appealing to his sense of 'justice', preaching love of 'one's fellow man', while at the same time they are really concerned with breaking down whatever remains of his character.

*   *   *

According to Rosenberg, Christian perversion of the old Nordic faith was a truly hideous thing. A cheerful, heroic, sunlit Mythus *was buried beneath papal Near-Eastern obscurantism.*

The Nordic gods were figures of light who bore spears, the cross and the swastika, and were crowned with haloes, symbols of the sun, of ascending life. It can be proved that, long before 3000 B.C., the Nordic *Volk*-waves bore these signs to Greece, Rome, Troy and India. Yet, Minutius Felix was greatly excited over the heathen cross. The final result was that the Roman (T-shaped) gibbet on which Jesus was slain had to be transformed into the heathen, now 'Christian' cross, and the heathen sun, particularly the heavenly cross, appeared as the haloes over the heads of Church martyrs and evangelists.*

The flash of lightning and the lance were transformed into divine symbols. The 'god on horseback' with his lance appeared again and again on 'Christian' memorials and designs. This was the eternal wanderer, Wotan, as he rode through the history of Christianity. Split up into many shapes, these gods lived and breathed as St Oswald, St George, St Martin and as armed horsemen. They lived throughout the Catholic lands as the holy affliction and even today as the 'Wode' they invisibly traverse the souls of the people of Lower Saxony. 'As long as a people lives, its gods are immortal.'† This was Wotan's revenge after his decline, until Balder arose from the dead and called himself saviour of the world.

Those in Rome, as well as in Wittenberg, were deeply distressed over the primal strength of the old Nordic tradition, one which 'Boniface' and his followers have been unable to annihilate, even to this day. However, there was nothing left to do but to transform the godly figures into Christian saints and to transfer their characteristics in a similar fashion.‡ However, the holidays of the

* In this context, we are witnessing the birth of a new science: the interpretation of old German symbols. The circle with four spokes appears as the heavenly cross, i.e. as the projection of directions from heaven; the six-part division indicates the points of summer and winter solstices, etc. *This* cosmic symbolism which, without ever being understood, was appropriated for an entire millennium, was the result of an age which represented its world of heavenly father, birth, death and eternity in symbols instead of with letters. The sun allegory represents a portion of this world picture.

† A. Dietrich, *Untergang der antiken Religion.*

‡ Numerous papal proclamations demonstrate how systematically this policy was carried out. Thus, for example, Pope Gregory 'the Great' wrote to Augustus, 'the Heathen' apostle, who asked his advice about conversion: 'For in our time [about A.D. 600] the Holy Church would certainly be able to turn many to the better through use of hot iron; others, however, it prefers to tolerate, but in such a fashion that they, because of this toleration and lack of attention, often suppress the evil with which they struggle' (Beda I, 27). And on July 22nd, A.D. 601, the same pope wrote to the Abbé

Christian Church fell on the same days as those celebrated
by the savages, whether this was the celebration of the
fertility goddess Ostara which became the celebration of
Christ's rising from the dead, or the celebration of the
winter solstice which was transformed into Jesus' birthday.
Thus, the Catholic Church in essence assumed the forms
of Northern Europe and was even influenced by the
Nordic race. What is grotesque here is the fact that it
attempted to transform need into a virtue while allowing
richness of spiritual life to be ascribed to itself. The enforced
belief of the Church explained all problems; every
nationality would have a place in the Church; every form
of piety stood under its protection. 'Nowhere else is
personal freedom of religious expression as well protected
as it is in the Catholic Church' (Adam). Naturally, this
is an all too clear reversal of the facts. 'Boniface', Louis
the Pious—who attempted to tear out root and branch
everything German—nine million murdered heretics,
even the Vatican Councils of today, are all animated by
the primary attempt to push through an inexorable unity
of spiritual belief (Unitarianism); to disseminate one
form, one compulsory belief, *one language* and *one* rite for
Nordic men, Levantines, niggers, Chinese and Eskimoes
(this is exemplified by the Eucharistic Congress in Chicago

Mellitus that if the heathen temples were not destroyed one could 'transform' them. 'If, then, the people does not see its temples destroyed, it will
dismiss its errors from its heart ... yet it might still prefer to find itself at the
accustomed places, hallowed by ancient wisdom.' And after permitting this
sacrifice, 'If several forms of external [*sic*] pleasure are allowed them, their
senses will become more quickly accustomed to joy from within. For it is
certainly not always the case that one is able to cut through hardened
souls; even those who aspire to climb the highest peak must do so one step at
a time ... and not plunge into the task all at once.' (Beda I, 30. Compare this
with T. Hänlein, *Die Bekehrung der Germanen zum Christentum* (Leipzig, 1914
and 1930, I, 57 and 64.)

in 1926, where nigger bishops celebrated the mass). For two thousand years the eternal blood of all races and peoples has revolted against this. However, just as the thought of world monarchy has exercised an hypnotic influence upon strong personalities from Alexander the Great to Napoleon, so also has the thought of a world-embracing, unified Church. And just as this former thought once brought millions under its spell, so also did the latter, without however being able to bring about complete internal submission to it. Therefore, the Roman Church counselled the great figures of the early Middle Ages to be allies, or at least accomplices, in the intrigues stemming from its romantic play for power. Moreover, the Church saw a weapon-bearing 'secular arm' as the means to clear a free path for its own spirit. If one applies the test of inner nature, this struggle turns out to be essentially one for domination by those who adhered to one of the following sets of values: love, humility, resignation and submission, or honour, dignity, self-assertion and pride.

Again: love was promoted and practised only by the *hangers-on* and *lower ranks* of the Roman system; the *leadership* needed in order to be durable and to be able to summon forth strong men, splendour, might and power over the souls and bodies of men. Without question a readiness for self-sacrifice has been nurtured by this system, which the Catholic Church, with pride, calls *caritas*. But even here in its most attractive humane effects a great difference is revealed between value and operation even in an ostensibly unified approach. Since the grace of God can only be mediated through the Church, so also are charity and compassion merely *gifts* of the Church to the unfortunate, to the sinner. Thus we have a very cleverly worked out system of recruitment, which is then applied to someone broken in spirit in order to bind him to a power-centre and to guide his conscience to recognize his complete nothingness before God and before that power which is represented by the Church triumphant. However, this line of thought lacks any of those qualities which we associate with nobility. Nordic people, conditioned by the concept of honour, could not be summoned in the name of a condescending love to extend communion to one in trouble; they would have to be summoned in the name of justice and duty. This would result not in submissive humility, but in an inner elevation; not in the shattering of personality, but in its strengthening, i.e. a reawakening of the consciousness of honour.

Also involved here is Christian-Church *sympathy*, which more recently has appeared in the form of freemasonic 'humanity' and which has led to the greatest devastation of our total life. Between the enforced belief in boundless love and the equality of all men before God on the one hand, and the teaching of democratic racelessness and of 'human rights' (ones which are not at all rooted in national concepts of honour) on the other, European society has assumed the role of protector of the inferior, sick, crippled, criminal and rotten. 'Love' plus 'humanity' has become a general rule which destroys all life-rules and life-forms of a people and state, and this has excited the present revenge of nature. A nation whose centre embodies honour and duty would not suffer laziness or criminality —it would expel it. We also can see in this example that a raceless scheme that lusts for unity is allied with unhealthy subjection, while a social and state community which is bound together through honour and duty does away with external difficulties out of a sense of justice, and the

consciousness of values on the part of those who belong
to the community makes them aware that this will
towards discipline must be an elevated one. Thus, even in
times of trouble, that which the Nordic life form is unable
to assimilate is excluded. If honour and the preservation of
the Nordic race which bears it are posited as the highest
values of all activity, then both of these phenomena will
emerge.

A typical example of how the Roman system uses
human weakness to its own advantage is found in the
compulsory belief in *indulgences* ... Proclaiming its 'divine
charge' to loose and to bind, the Church considers the
account of the Saviour from the point of view of the
respective sinner (it was the African Tertullian who
expounded this shopkeeper precept with much expendi-
ture of legalistic sophistry). The Church has attempted to
surround this precept with obscurantist elucidation and
has constructed an entire philosophy on the basis of this
vicarious atonement. However, its mercenary substratum
will not remain hidden to a perceptive individual. It is
mercenary with regard to spiritual as well as to material
relationships. In principle, the idea of indulgence is based
upon an example of reckoning in which the Church is
ultimately responsible for providing for an unknown x or y
with whatever reparations figure it desires. This breeds
chaos in both character and soul, quite apart from the
external consequences which resulted from this practice
by the time of Luther—when a business representative of
the Fuggers always accompanied the upright Tetzel[1] and
took all incoming money off his hands, because the

[1] The Fuggers were an important banking family in 15th- and 16th-
century Italy. The Church was sometimes in debt to them. Johann Tetzel
(1465–1519) was a German monk who sold papal indulgences. His activities
aroused the anger of Martin Luther. (Ed.)

indebted pope would not pay the Augsburg shopkeeper.[2]
The dogma of indulgence was possible only because the
concept of a personal feeling of honour had entered into
its formulation. Further, it amounted to an undermining
of that existing consciousness of honour and a concurrent
designation of servility as being synonymous with piety.
Viewed externally, the German rebellion against this
scandal has compelled the Roman Church to be more
careful in implementing the abuse of indulgence. However, it is still defended in principle by today's Church as a
justified and pious practice (see the General Proclamation
on Indulgence of 1926). It is self-explanatory that this
nonsense is traced back to 'biblical justification'. So
effective has been the millennium-old chastisement
inflicted by Rome upon the non-Nordic substratum of
European peoples, that this appeal to shattered humanity
has been received not as an insult, but as accepted aid
from those of the Body of Christ.

* * *

*The external corruption of the Church only reflected its inner
degradation, which was brought about by its acceptance of the
Old Testament and the notion it contained of an all-powerful
terrible and capricious God. As we will see, Rosenberg considers it
a weakness on the part of Martin Luther that, while he recognized
the perfidy of the Jews, he never rejected the Old Testament.*

The remote and fearful God, enthroned over all; this
is Jahweh of the so-called Old Testament, a God to whom
one prays in fear and praises in trembling. He created all

---

[2] A long footnote condemning the 'Jubilee Year' of the Church as being
simply a money-making device has been omitted. (Ed.)

of us out of nothing and if it suits Him He decrees magical
miracles and constructs a world for His own glorification.
This Syrian-African superstition, despite fire and sword,
could never be forced upon Europeans. In fact, the
Nordic spiritual inheritance comprised consciousness not
only of the divinity of the human soul, but of its *equality*
with God. The Indian teaching of the equality of Atman
and Brahman — 'The Universe is Being, because he
himself is in the Universe' — was the first great recognition
of this knowledge. The Persian teaching of the shared
struggle of men and of Ahura Mazda reveals to us the
rough-hewn, Nordic-Iranian conception; the Greek
pantheon was descended from a soul as great as that
which produced the autocratic, Idea-doctrines of Plato.
The old Germanic conception of God is simply unthinkable
without spiritual freedom. And even Jesus spoke of the
kingdom of heaven *within* us. The wilfulness of spiritual
seeking was already revealed in Odin, the world-traveller,
is revealed in Eckhart, seeker and confessor, and is
displayed by all great men from Luther to Lagarde.
Unfortunately, Rome, being Syrian-Near-Eastern and
Judaic in character, opted for Jahweh.

Rome-Jahweh means: the despotism of magic; the
miraculous creation from nothing (a thought which is
nonsensical for us). The Nordic West maintains that:
Ego and God are spiritual polarities; that each act of
creation is a completed amalgamation; that diffusion calls
forth renewed dynamic strengths. The true Nordic soul is
always embarked on a soaring flight 'to' and 'from' God.
Its 'peace in God' is synonymous with 'peace in itself'.
This unification, which is simultaneously felt as bequeath-
ment and self-consciousness is the Nordic mystique.
Roman 'mystique' means essentially the impossible

requirement that one abandons polarity and dynamic; it means the subjugation of humanity. Roman philosophy does not stand apart, as it maintains it does, from the three typical orientations of soul: immanence, transcendence and transcendentalism. It embraces all of them, while representing a compromise attempt to bind portions of all of these types to Judeo-Syrian-African beliefs. Roman precepts do not stem from *one* centre and flow in a thousand streams through the world. Rather, their Syrian essence is disguised in uncontroversial and falsified precepts of Nordic man as he constructed his world of thought in the form of different *Volkish* personalities. The attitude towards the problem of *Dasein* and *Sosein* stems from this.[3]

The Judaic-Roman teachings, through maintaining that God created the world from nothing, preach a causal connection between 'creation' and 'created'. In so doing they transfer a form of perception which is valid only for this world to the region of metaphysics, while still maintaining this presupposition of theirs—i.e. their 'vicarious' position *vis-à-vis* the Creator—up to this day and with tenacious energy, in that they are conscious of the fact that their battle for existence is being waged at this level. The German spirit has always stood in sharpest opposition towards this monstrous principle. Even the oldest of the Nordic creation myths, the Indian, does not recognize Nothingness. It recognizes a well-established tradition which speaks of chaos. It conceives of the cosmos as originating from an order principle which struggles against chaos. For a moment this tradition also conceives

[3] Here, Rosenberg is employing a differentiation between Being *as given* (*Sosein*) and existence (*Dasein*) 'there' (DA) Being. He is indicating that Judaic-Roman teachings posit a world as given by the Creator while *existence* (*Dasein*), precedes and *conditions* Being as given. (Ed.)

of an orderer from the outside (not of creation from nothing!); however, after posing the question of the origin of creation, the tradition concludes with the highest degree of philosophical discretion:

> He, who has called forth creation
> who gazes upon it in the highest heavenly light
> who has made it or not made it
> who knows of it!—or does even he not know?

Indian monism really stemmed from a sharp dualism: the soul alone is of essence, all matter is an illusion which must be overcome. A *creation* of this matter, even if it were from nothing, would appear to the Indian Aryan to be blasphemous materialism. In the Indian creation myth, a frame of mind similar to that of Hellas and of the Germans is revealed: chaos ordered itself according to a will, a law; but the world *never* originated from Nothingness, as was taught by Syrian-African sons of the wasteland and as Rome has accepted it in the form of the daemon Jahweh. Schiller's saying, 'If I think of God, I relinquish the creation,' signifies in briefest form the clear rejection by the Aryan-Nordic race-soul of that miraculous-magical union of 'creator and created' as being that of God and worthless creature. Rome has kneaded together Isis, Horus, Jahweh, Plato, Aristotle, Jesus, St Thomas and so on, and wants to force this *Sosein* upon the *Dasein* of the races and peoples or, if this does not work, it seeks to instil, drop by drop, ingratiating falsification in order to cripple the natural-grown Being of nature; these spiritual and racial cripples will then be collected under the Catholic roof.

Up to now, only a very few have opposed their type-creating strengths against this grandiose attempt to

annihilate peoples. One of the greatest rejected the
Roman medicine-man philosophy; the other fought it
because of what it was; the third concerned himself with
other issues. Systematic protection of Europe from this
extensive attack has, in great measure, nowhere yet begun.
Unfortunately, Lutheranism, in spite of its 'protesting',
has been an accomplice of Rome. For the Lutheran
'belief' in justice so far has shut it off from life, because of
its oath upon the Jewish Bible. It preached a *Sosein*,
without directing itself back towards the organic *Dasein*.
Finally, today, there is occurring a fundamental awakening from this power hypothesis: we are not confronting
life from the point of view of an enforced principle that
is still of Jewish-Roman-African ancestry. Rather, we
seek to determine *Sosein* from *Dasein* (as Meister Eckhart
once longed to do). This *Dasein*, however, is the race-
bound soul with its highest values of honour and spiritual
freedom, values which determine the constructive division
of the other values. This race-soul lives and unfolds itself
in nature, a nature which awakens certain characteristics
while inhibiting others. These strengths of race, soul and
nature are the eternal preconditions, *Dasein* and life, and
it is only from them that *Sosein* is finally produced as civilization, forms of belief, art and so on. This is the last, inner
transformation, the newly awakening *Mythus* of our life.

That great man of longing, Paracelsus—Theophrastus
of Hohenheim—would also speak in this way if he lived
today among us. He stood awakened, in a world of
bloated, abstract scholars, enemies of the *Volk*; individuals
who, armed with glued-together doctrines from Greece,
Rome and Arabia, poisoned the living body of man, made
the sick sicker and, in spite of quarrelling among themselves, stood together as a wall against any genius who

strove searchingly upward towards the course of *Dasein*. To investigate Nature in the totality of her laws; to value medicine as a necessary means of extending the life processes of the body and not as an isolated magical lucky-dip: these were the motives which drove Theophrastus of Hohenheim through the world of his time as a lonely prophet—restless, hated and feared. He was stamped with genius, and viewed not even church and altar, teachings and maxim as ends in themselves, but valued them only to the degree that they were imbedded in the milieu of nature and blood. The great Paracelsus thus became a spokesman for all German scientists and German mystics; a great preacher of *Dasein*. Like Meister Eckhart, he reached about and rose to the stars while, with a mixture of pride and humility, he conformed to the great laws of the universe, filled with as much bliss by the purity of the nightingale's call as by the inexpressible creative tremor of his own heart.

... Odin was and is dead. However, the German mystic discovered this 'strength from above' in his own soul. Divine Valhalla arose from the infinite, misty-vastness buried in the human breast. This discovery and the preaching of imperishable freedom of soul constituted the saving grace which, until today, has protected us against all attempts at suppression. Thus, the religious history of the West has been, almost exclusively, a history of religious rebellion. True religion *within* the Church (as in the case of the saintly Francis and Fra Angelico) existed only to the degree that the unfolding of the Nordic soul could not be hindered—because its echoes in Western man were still too strong.

The new, reborn German man—albeit clad in the garments of his time—appeared on the scene in the form of the German mystic. The spiritual birth of our culture was not culminated in the time of the so-called Renaissance, nor in the so-called Reformation — these were more ages of external disintegration and despairing struggle. No, the idea of spiritual personality, the supportive idea of our history, became a religious and life precept for the first time in the thirteenth and fourteenth centuries. Also, at this time the essence of our later, critical philosophy was deliberately discovered and was preached in the form of the eternal metaphysical creed of the Nordic West. Indeed, this creed had been alive in the souls of many races. However, it could not be generally accepted until the time was ripe for it. 'The deepest spring bears the highest crest.' It is the legacy of our age that we sink — submerge unto the deepest depths so that the highest can be elevated to the light. Only the age itself can reveal if it is worthy of this calling.

It was over three hundred years before the name of Christ meant anything to the peoples of the Mediterranean. About a thousand more years had to pass before all of the West became familiar with Him. When Confucius died, he was mourned by only a few. Veneration of him began only three hundred years after his death. The first temple was built to him five hundred years later. Today, he is prayed to as 'the completely saintly' in 1,500 temples. Similarly, six hundred years passed over the grave of Meister Eckhart before the German soul could comprehend him. Today, a light is dawning within the *Volk*, a light that shows that the time is now ripe for the apostle of the Germans, the 'holy and blissful Meister'.*

* It is an eternal shame that Meister Eckhart still has not been given a thorough and creative examination. The Pfeiffer firm edited his sermons. The writings of Denifle offer the best example of what Catholic publishers did to Eckhart. The great German is reduced to a level beneath the position

Each creative being is driven towards a goal which is perhaps unknown even to him. The soul also has a goal: to be true to itself and to attain consciousness of God. However, in the world of the senses, of space and of time, this soul has been 'dispersed and scattered'. The senses activate themselves within the soul and—first of all— weaken its coherence. The prerequisite for the 'inner work' is, therefore, the retraction of all strengths which strive towards the external; the extinguishing of all symbols and similes. However, this 'inner work' means to grasp the kingdom of heaven within oneself, as Jesus had attested to and required when He spoke of 'rulers' of the soul. Thus, this attempt of the mystics demanded the elimination of the world as idea, in order to make us as conscious as possible that we were pure subject[s] of a metaphysical essence that dwelt within us. Since this is not *completely* possible, the idea of 'God' was created as a new object of the soul, this finally leading to the proclamation that soul and God were of equal value.

This act is possible only under the precondition of

---

of imitator, whose caperings are 'repulsive'. See Denifle's *Meister Eckharts lat. Schriften* (1886), particularly 'The Spiritual Life', a collection full of saccharine and religious twaddle in which Eckhart supposedly participated. P. Mehlhorn gives only a short survey which says little (*Die Blütezeit der deutschen Mystik*), while A. Spamer has collected some interesting texts (*Texte aus der deutschen Mystik des 14. und 15. Jahrhunderts*). O. Karrer's 1923 selected texts of Meister Eckhart are most instructive. Dr A. Dempf's investigation in his life, *Metaphysik des Mittelalters*, is somewhat tiresome, but contains some insights into the great Eckhart. H. Büttner has produced both the best work and the deepest evaluation: *Meister Eckhart's Schriften und Predigten*, 2 vols. I have followed his rendering of Eckhart, which is very clear. It is hoped that the firm of E. Diedrichs, Jena, will publish a quite reasonable and perhaps shortened popular form of the *Works*. It belongs in every German home as indispensable literature. I have heard that the editing of the collected works of Eckhart has been in progress since 1931. It is about time!

freedom of soul from all dogmas, churches and popes. And Meister Eckhart, the Dominican priest, did not hesitate to preach joyfully and publicly this basic credo of all Aryan Beings. Throughout his long life, he spoke of the 'unoriginated and uncreatable light of the soul', and preached, 'God has granted free determination to the soul, so that He will do nothing beyond thine own free will nor will He force upon it that which it does not want.' In opposition to all principles of compulsion, he went on to declare that there were three elements which testified to the 'noble soul'. 'The first involved the glory of the Being (that "heavenly" agent). The second concerns the potency of its strength, and the third, the fecundity of its works.' Before each 'going out' into the world, the soul had to become conscious of 'its unique beauty'. However, the *inner* task of conquering the kingdom of heaven can only be completed through the highest degree of freedom. 'Thy soul will bear no fruit until thou hast accomplished thy task, and neither God nor thyself will abandon thee if thou hast brought thine to the world. Otherwise, thou wilt have no peace and thou wilt bear no fruit. And even then, it is still disquieting enough, because it is born from a soul which is bound (to the outside world) and whose tasks are controlled; not from a soul born in freedom.' And if the question is posed as to why God had become man, the heretic Eckhart does not answer, because then we poor miserable sinners could have an abundance of good works to which we could ascribe. Rather, he said, 'I answer: so that God will be born in the soul ... ' Out of this there arose the joyous credo: 'The soul in which God should be born must forsake time, and time must forsake it: it must rise upwards and stand completely strengthened in the kingdom of God; this is breadth and width which is neither broad nor wide. There, the soul knows all things, and knows them in their totality.' Also, the Master wrote this as wide as the heavens: '*The smallest power that there is in my soul is wider than the width of heaven!*' ... Thus, if one recognizes the 'noble soul' as being the *highest* value, as the axis around which everything is directed, the ideas of love, humility, compassion, grace and so on will sink to second or third rank. And even here, Eckhart did not hesitate to listen to the voice of this 'little spark' and to speak out unconcernedly what *his* soul told him. Naturally, it need not be emphasized that he did not deprecate love, or humility, or compassion or the teachings of grace. We often find in his sermons the most beautiful phrases concerning these ideas. However, he hated saccharine ecstasies, drowsy 'beautiful feelings' — in short, all spiritual instability. His teaching of love represents it as strength; one which knows that it is *equal* to those divine powers which rage about it. Love must 'break through the thing'; for only 'a spirit that has become free can force God to itself'. We must realize what it meant for a Dominican priest to undertake, at the beginning of the fourteenth century and in the face of an intolerant Church which ruled the world, a transmutation of all the most treasured values; yes, and even dare to attempt to transmit a positive, *new* highest value to the humble faithful. This could not have taken the form of an open attack on Rome, but only of a plastic, positive depiction of spiritual experiences. Bearing this in mind, we read Eckhart's sermon on the 'Loneliness of Soul', perhaps the most beautiful testimony to German consciousness of personality.

In it, Eckhart is dealing with the highest values of the

Christian Church—love, humility and compassion—and discovers that these qualities must yield, in stature, depth and greatness, to that of the soul, which stands by itself alone. He combated Paul's singular glorification of love, for the best that love can do is to make us love God. However, it is of much greater significance that we are drawn to God and draw God to us, because then our soul will be comforted to be at one with God. God's own abode is in unity and purity. However, these in turn reside in isolation. 'Therefore, God cannot help but to surrender Himself to lonely hearts.' Furthermore, the suffering in the world which results in love always applies to creatures. With spiritual isolation, this situation no longer pertains. With isolation, the world is reduced to nothingness and this brings us closer to God. With regard to humility, man lowers his soul to the level of creatures when he practises it, thus losing something of himself. 'No matter how splendid such a departure might be, that which remains inward is always something so much higher.' 'Complete isolation of soul brooks no imitation of creatures, no self-humiliation nor self-elevation; it strives to be neither below nor above, wanting only to rest in itself, reaching neither towards love nor towards suffering. It does not consider its equality or inequality with other beings; it wants neither the one nor the other. *It wants only to be at one with itself.*'

Probably nowhere else has the aristocratic soul been made so explicit as here. Respect for oneself, the necessary counter-balance to recognition of fruitful activity was later treasured by Goethe as the highest of all gospels.

According to Eckhart, compassion is nothing other than an abandoning of self. For this reason, therefore, it is not treasured as highly nor seen as being as valuable as isolation. However, because God's Being also constitutes an isolated phenomenon, it follows that everything external to Him could not be absorbed. From this point of view, Eckhart imposes severe limitations upon the efficacy of prayer, so often clothed in magic nonsense, and its significance. 'I maintain that all prayer and all good works will disturb His loneliness as little as if they were nothing, and God will be as little inclined or as merciful towards man as He would be if no prayer had been offered and no good works done.' This is more than plain: it is a complete rejection of the magic-ensconced, interceding Church, of its 'representative' and 'saving' capacities. A *Volkish* credo then follows in conclusion:

Preserve thy loneliness from all men; remain undisturbed by all accepted impression. *Free thyself from anything that could be foreign to thy being* and direct thy conscience towards the salutory view by which thou bearest God in thine heart, as an object from which thine eyes never wander.

III. *KULTUR:* THE *VOLKISH* AESTHETIC

Rosenberg naturally saw art as reflective of the organic Volk-*soul.*
A strange and perhaps significant parallel can be drawn between
the aesthetic of Rosenberg and the aesthetic(s) of that modern
art which he defamed as 'degenerate'. The Volkish *aesthetic*
and that of the modern artist were both reactions to the atomization
of man in a technical world. The modern artist sought either to
restructure this world, e.g. in the case of Cubism, or radically to
individualize it through non-representational art. Rosenberg's
reaction against the factory-world of the twentieth century was to
offer an aesthetic by virtue of which the alienated individual
artist or spectator could snugly ensconce himself in the warm-
hearted collectivity of a timeless Volk-Mythus. *The following*
extracts are taken from Der Mythus des 20. Jahrhunderts.

Almost all philosophers who have written about the
'aesthetic condition' or about the fixation of values in art,
have come to accept the fact of a racial beauty ideal
which is applied to physical observation, and also of a
unified highest ideal that infuses art, in a spiritual manner.
Therefore, it is obvious that if anything at all can be said
about the essence and efficacy of art, the purely physical
representation of a Greek, for example, will make a far
different impression upon us than a picture of a Chinese
Emperor. Each outline, as conceived in China, has a
different function from that of the Greeks, a function
which can be neither explained nor 'aesthetically enjoyed'
without knowledge of the formative, racially-determined

Will. Every work of art embodies spiritual content. Outside formal investigation, even this can be understood only on the basis provided by observing different race-souls. As a whole, our current aesthetic—in spite of many minor corrections—has met with no response. Yet the naive, as well as the conscious, true artist, has always proceeded in a race-constructive manner, and he has embodied externally spiritual peculiarities, through utilizing those racial types that surrounded him, types which, in the first place, became the exceptional bearers of certain characteristics.

... The Greek as hero ... is represented in equal measure not only in Hellenic plastic art, but also in decorative art; in vase-painting, his lean body is representative of the modern ideal of beauty; however, in profile, he is more softly-drawn than the later German. Besides the great Hellenic art, we gaze upon the vase-paintings of Exikias, Clitias and Nikosthenes. We see, for example, how Exikias depicts Ajax and Achilles playing at dice, and we see his Castor with the horses; we see the Hydras of the Charitaios with the Amazons; the blonde wife of Euphronius on the Cylix of Orpheus, which seems to have a certain Gretchen-quality about it; the imperious Aphrodite with the goose;* the crater of Naples of Aristophanes and Ergines, and so on. In thousands of vases and craters we find a similarly-constructed type which changes very little, a type which obviously attributes the excitement of the heroic, the beautiful and the great to the Greeks alone. However, in opposition to this, a conscious racial contrast has been established; for example, in the representations of daemons, satyrs and centaurs. Thus, the Cylix of Phineas, found on the islands, has three representations of male wantonness

* On this see E. Pfuhl, *Malerei und Zeichnung der Griechen*, p. 498.

with all its attributes. The heads of the three are round and fat, the forehead swollen to the proportions of a hydrocephalic, the nose short and bulbous, the lips protruding. Andokides depicted the daemon in exactly the same manner, showing him to be hairy and with a long beard; also visible is the profile of the fleshy, thick neck. The same type is brilliantly represented in Cleophrades,* where a fully conscious sense of racial contrast is revealed in the skull shapes depicted in the true Greek Bacchante. In precisely the same manner, Nikosthenes plainly shows the satyr who, as the wine-bearer, is an animalistic, idiotic caricature; while Euphronius has left us a daemon Cylix, which clearly illustrates the obtuse, hairy-negroid-Eastern racial type. Besides these two predominant contrasts—the lean, strong, aristocratic Greek and the short, stunted, animalistic daemon (a type which unquestionably was associated with a race that was subjugated and now enslaved by the Greeks)—besides these, we can see Asiatic-type figures in these paintings; figures which accompanied the gradual trickling-in of Asian blood, and which are also depicted as being Semitic or Jewish. A bowl of Eosmeister, for example shows us a Semitic tradesman with a pack on his back while a Harpy has been drawn upon the early, lower-Italian crater of Phineus, a Harpy whose head and hand movements can be marvelled at *in natura* on the *Kurfürstendamm* today.[1]

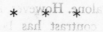

After disposing of the Asian elements so negatively prominent

---

* Op. cit. p. 379.

[1] Kurfürstendamm is one of the main thoroughfares of Berlin. (Ed.)

in Greek art (ugly Socrates himself is described by Rosenberg as pointing to the decay of Greece! See Mythus, *pp.* 280–88*), Rosenberg turns to a more thorough discussion of the Greek-Nordic beauty ideal. Before we examine his view of this ideal, we would do well to recognize that, in deprecating Socrates, Rosenberg might have been taking his cue from Nietzsche who, of course, was also an enemy of Socrates and the Socratic method.*

...Collective Europe's hero-ideal is synonymous with a tall, lean figure with shining eyes, high forehead, muscular but not muscle-bound. A hero represented as squat, broad-shouldered, bow-legged, bull-necked and with a flattened forehead is a contradiction in terms, and this type can be found only when people like Ebert[2] have come to the surface. We need only examine the heads of the Hohenstaufen kings, the monument in Magdeburg and the head of Henry II. For example, we observe how Rethel himself depicts the face of Charlemagne; how also his opponent Widukind has been described; we read how Old France describes Roland, what Wolfram tells us about Parsifal. We need only consider all this to know that here inner and outer being has been inextricably tied together in a spiritual-racial unity, and to understand how this—in a thousand forms—produces that which we experience as great art whenever it appears. The St George of Donatello reveals in its calmness the same beauty ideal as the Gattamelata, indeed even the same ideal as is found in the wild, distorted expression of Colleoni. The Duke of Wellington and Gustavus Adolphus are separated from von Moltke only by hair-style and type of beard. Here, however, we must note a change from earlier times: earlier the hero and field-marshal personally

[2] Leading Social Democrat and first President of the Weimar Republic (1919–25). (Ed.)

led his people into battle; the *whole* person was therefore a symbol. Today, a more internalized dynamic predominates: will and brain, drawing upon a centre, direct millions. Because of this, the whole figure is often depicted less than the head alone. Its depiction makes possible for us a stronger concentration on that which is most essential. Forehead, nose, eyes, mouth and chin become bearers of a will, of a particular direction of thought. The path from the static to the dynamic is recognizable here. It is at this point that Nordic-Western art is differentiated from the Greek Ideal.

... Greece represents race-determined beauty in the externalized staticness of the Nordic race; the Nordic West represents racially-unique beauty as an inner dynamic. The face of Pericles and the head of Frederick the Great are two symbols of the polarities within the race-soul, and of an ideal of racial beauty which was originally one and the same.

*   *   *

Rosenberg gives several examples of Nordic art.

It is shameful and yet true that while there are aestheticians without number, the indispensable precondition for an aesthetic, a study of the development of the racial beauty ideal, until now, has never been written.* Laymen, art scholars and even the artists themselves trudge along with closed eyes through the galleries, read European and Chinese poetry without grasping their true essence and the actual laws of form. It is here that the Northern soul makes itself felt. People merely cast a glance at one of the

---

* Up to now, statements on this can be found only in Günther's *Rassenkunde* and in Schultze-Naumburg's *Kunst und Rasse*.

most revered works of European painting, Eyck's Triptych
with the singing children.[3] Again and again, the work of
Eyck reiterates the common representative ideal of Nordic
men — technically and in drawing he had not quite
attained the heights achieved by later artists; however,
in his inner feeling for form he was their equal. The
youthful head in the left-hand portion of the painting
(from the point of view of the observer) — in the manner in
which it is detached from the background — represents the
purest racial beauty, and his counterpart with furrowed
brow is revealed in the face of God in the upper-middle
portion. A similar spirit animates the Eyck head in the
Berlin museum. To pursue this more deeply: the God
which Michelangelo uses to awaken Adam to life reveals
the same *typus* as does the head of God that appears in
Van Eyck's work, even though Michelangelo most
certainly did not have even a suspicion of the essence of
Eyck's creation. However, the same head appears (even
if somewhat altered by spiritual tension) in the figure of
Moses, who is shaking with rage. The Dutch painters, as
well as the Italian, discovered that it was possible to
represent powerful grandeur in only *one* typical manner.
Neither Jan van Eyck nor Michelangelo could embody
their ideals of majesty, strength and honour in the
countenance of the Jewish race. One only has to visualize
a face with hooked nose, drooping lips, piercing black
eyes and wool hair to understand the plastic impossibility
of embodying the European God in a Jewish face (to say
nothing of the Jewish body). This insight also suffices to
show why even the *inner* God-idea of Judaism — which,
together with the Jewish external form constitutes *one*
essence — has to be completely rejected. *Here*, however, our

[3] Rosenberg was referring to Jan van Eyck (1385?–1440). (Ed.)

race has been poisoned by Judaism; the means for this
being the Bible and the Church of Rome. With their
help, that wasteland daemon became the 'God' of Europe.
Whoever refused to accept Him was burned or poisoned.
*Only through art did Western man save himself, and he created
his divinity in pictures and from stone. In spite of the tragic
struggle which it entailed, he sought to realize this inner beauty in
colours and in marble, while placing this treasure at the disposal
of a spirit which not one European artist could embody as God or
even as beauty.*

... Rembrandt was a good Bible scholar (or, to put it
more accurately, he seldom read the Bible itself, but
rather, he almost always illustrated stories from Jacob
Cat's Dutch folk book *Trouringh*); therefore, he felt
obliged to paint many Jewish heads in order to represent
'correctly' biblical stories. He painted Joseph .as he,
gesturing, protested his 'innocence' — after being caught
red-handed — to the husband of Potiphar, whom he had
attacked (Berlin). However, as soon as Rembrandt became
concerned with serious matters, he left the Amsterdam
ghetto. The father of 'The Lost Son' (Petersburg) is
stripped of all Jewish attributes: we see a tall, Nordic
old man, with spiritual, good hands. The precision of the
Nordic-Italian artist was foreign to Rembrandt. He strove
not so much after line, but rather atmosphere, earthly
symphonies of colour, and the mysterious. In spite of this,
his 'Christ in Emmaus' (Paris) is just as much a heartfelt
Nordic as is the painting of his mother (Petersburg) and
the splendid figure of Danaë (Petersburg) shows that even
Rembrandt could not paint true beauty any differently
from that manner in which it inundated the soul of
Giorgione. One of the tenderest paintings of Rembrandt
is called 'Jewish Bride', and it is a compelling fact that

even here, every blemish of Jewish 'beauty' has had to yield to a coarse but tender Nordic feeling.

*   *   *

Rosenberg also evinced a concern for music. His attitude towards the Nordic folk-soul as reflected in music is represented best in Rosenberg's considerations of two musicians, Ludwig van Beethoven and Richard Wagner. The essay 'Beethoven' appeared in the March 26th, 1927, issue of the Völkischer Beobachter, *and is taken from* Blut und Ehre, ein Kampf für deutsche Wiedergeburt, Reden und Aufsätze von 1919–1933, *herausgegeben von Thilo von Trotha (München,* 1939*).*

BEETHOVEN

It gives one a striking feeling to realize that while a totally aroused world gazes upon Germany with hostile eyes, March 26th will be solemnized in all lands and cities which claim devotion to culture as a day of remembrance for one of the very greatest of the same German people. On the hundredth anniversary of his death, hundreds of thousands are listening to his music, millions are reading about him in newspapers and magazines and, even in Paris and Warsaw, words about German culture will be heard again. Like some primeval giant, Beethoven subdues and captivates the human heart even today; really, more today than ever before. Today, the whole world is in ferment and strives for the wilful, the titanic.

Two human types emerge from all the great figures of the German West. One type wants to conquer the secret of life from all *sides*, as one would storm an encircled fortress; it seeks to subdue the secret through a world-embracing strategy. This was the intellectual, spiritual position of a Leonardo, a Descartes, a Kant, a Leibniz and a Goethe.

In all of them there dwelt the longing for a universality of the all-embracing spirit, a *universal* striving and exploration.

The other type approaches the secret of Being with doubled energy, but from only *one* side. He wants to take the fortress by storm in order to lay bare its innermost contents. This was the primary drive in Michelangelo, in Rembrandt, in Schopenhauer and in Richard Wagner. Beethoven also belongs to the second type: 'he grabbed fate by the throat', and he recognized that, above all other qualities, strength was distinguished as the moral of man. In its spiritual struggle, our age needs a slow, strategic method less than it does a one-sided, impatient engagement. When the old values shatter and new ones are born, all strengths, in accordance with nature, wilfully collect themselves against several small points and finally against *one* strong point. As certain as we are that, after the victory, there will again be a time of rhythmic relaxation, and that the Epicurean and 'classicist' will again be able to work anew, we are equally certain that today, single-minded moderation of will is the first order of business.

And because of this, no single day of remembrance, of the many which we celebrate, is as capable of releasing as deep powers as the day of the hundredth anniversary of the death of Ludwig van Beethoven. Whoever has grasped that Being which lives in our movement, whoever knows that a similar impulse lives in all of us, knows that Beethoven embodies this to the highest possible degree. The dashing forward over the ruins of a shattered world; the hope for a new world-shaping will; the strong joy that shines through the most passionate of tragedies —

> Run your course with joy, brother
> as a hero to the victory ...

Thus resounds the highest point of the Ninth Symphony.

For one day we will permit ourselves consciousness of the heart-warming fact that Beethoven the German moves *all* Western peoples, and that the best among them treasure him as a centre of true creativity. However, we want also to remind ourselves that Beethoven can and must give to us the driving will for German solidarity. *For today, we live in the Eroica of the German people.*

*   *   *

As might be expected, Richard Wagner was an object of primary interest for Rosenberg, much as he was for Adolf Hitler. Rosenberg, however, endeavoured to arrive at a 'scientific' understanding of this perplexing genius. The following extracts are taken from Der Mythus des 20. Jahrhunderts.

... The greatest conscious attempt to awaken, with all visual and aural means, the sublimity of the will, was to be found in Wagner's *music-drama*. Wagner declared that the dance, music and poetry were one art, and he traced the divisiveness and sterility of his own time back to the fact that each of the arts had in itself succeeded in pressing to the very limits of productivity and was now tearing itself apart. Beethoven's absolute music led to this insight, which is reflected in the Ninth Symphony, where he returns to the human voice. If rhythm is the skeleton of tone, the human voice is its flesh. By itself, though, music lacked 'moral will', and its parochialism led either to chaos or to hollow programme music. Drama, estranged from both music and dance, was the most complete embodiment of the lyrical art. However, after it is detached from the 'other' arts, it of necessity culminates in self-enclosed tragedies which can never be represented. In such a way did Goethe miscarry, as did so many of his followers. Thanks to this fragmentation, the dance—which was originally genuine and alive only as national dance, combined with folk-music and song—had now become an unnatural movement of the legs, without form and true rhythm. Wagner saw the art-mode of the future as being a union of the three arts, one which would result in 'tone-and-word drama'.

Wagner fought against a totally vulgarized world and won; unquestionably, the cultural achievements of Bayreuth will stand for eternity. However, there is today a turning away from the Wagnerian principle that dance, music and poetry *always* have to be unified, and that this had to be done, as though Bayreuth represented an unchangeable completion of the Aryan mystique.

*   *   *

Rosenberg was critical of Wagner in one significant way: he felt that Wagner had underestimated the relationship between motor-excitement and the will.

For a while, i.e. when the sensualist-psychological aesthetic dominated the field, people exaggerated the importance of this motor factor. However, the 'classical' reaction has pressed this factor too far into the background. That clarion call to battle, the 'Hohenfriedburg March', to whose strains millions have marched to their deaths, shows how heroic, blaring sound can nurture a physical will which expends itself in great physical energy. The rhythm of the true national dance, to which sound a given people responds both emotionally and physically, is also involved here. Also, time and space stand in a determined relationship which can be limited by no third factor. If, however, word-drama, music and dance-music are brought together simultaneously, without even the briefest pause, it is impossible to avoid artistic discord. We have often made light of the opera in which a hero announces his flight and yet remains standing for ten minutes. However, in Wagner's dramas also, the inner harmony between word-content and gesture is often hindered by the music. For example, when Brünhilde suddenly sees Siegfried in Gunther's castle and rushes passionately to him, the words of her song restrict the course of her movement. Siegfried, on the other hand, has to complete a defensive gesture almost in slow motion. The same applies to most of the scenes between the gods and the giants in *Rheingold*.

In these cases, the music—bearing in mind its physical possibilities—disturbs the course of emotional and physical responses; in other cases, the words cannot follow the rapidity of the dance. Thus, we must admit to falsification here also, an occurrence which, to be sure, very seldom happens in the music-dramas.

These observations are not a critique of trifling matters. Rather, they are based on a phenomenon of which Wagner himself and every opera-singer has been most certainly and most painfully aware: *that the three arts cannot be fused for very long*, but that, as in earlier times, when they stood apart from one another, their respective intrinsic peculiarities cannot be violated without inflicting serious damage upon the arts. The attempt to push through this unification destroyed the spiritual rhythm and hindered physical motor expression and impression. Here, Wagner, whose art represents a singularly tremendous effort of will, occasionally gets in his own way. The preconditions of his greatness also produced the conditions for his own weakness. Most people who listen to the Wagnerian music-drama sense this without being able to explain their displeasure. However, the incomparable impressions engendered by the mystical-heroic scenes outweigh this darkly-felt incongruity between space and time ... * In making these observations, we have in no way diminished Wagner's achievement. It bore witness to *life*, and this is decisive. It was certainly also blessed in that it brought together completely different art forms. They have all mutually benefited from this. Perhaps there will come some day another great man who, reaching into the core of life and bearing in mind newly realized laws of uniqueness for the three arts, will present us with a new form of the tone-and-word drama using 'Egmont' and *Tristan* as prototypes. *However, the most essential of all the strengths of Western art had become manifest in Richard Wagner: That the Nordic soul is not contemplative and that it does not lose itself in individual psychology, but that it wilfully experiences cosmic-spiritual laws and is architectonically constructed.* Richard Wagner is one of those artists who embodies each of the three factors which constitute our collective aesthetic life: the Nordic beauty ideal, as it has been externalized in *Lohengrin* and *Siegfried*, an ideal which is linked to the deepest feeling for nature; the inner wilfulness of men, as this is revealed in *Tristan und Isolde*; and the struggle over that high value of Nordic-Western man, hero-honour com-

---

* I offer as an observation my conviction that Wagner, in the *Ring* places such great demands on men and on theatre, that they simply cannot follow his great effort. Also, some of the symbolic effects (*Ring, Parsifal*) are too technical. Even if the reproduction of the classic Walpurgis is completely abandoned, we will never be able satisfactorily to render the *Ring*. While Tristan and Hans Sachs have eternal life, the *Ring* will either have to be completely reformed by a similarly gifted hand, or it will gradually disappear from the theatre.

bined with an inner truthfulness. This inner beauty idea is developed in Wotan, in King Mark and in Hans Sachs (*Parsifal* represents a church-influenced enfeeblement in favour of the value of renunciation).

*   *   *

As might be expected, Rosenberg showed an interest in Nietzsche. In an interesting address on October 14th, 1944,[4] *the hundredth anniversary of Nietzsche's birth, Rosenberg utilized selected writings of his to bolster the somewhat strained German war effort. The writings used give a self-consciously distorted picture of Nietzsche. The latter's contempt for the German people and German nationalism, which can be found in* Nietzsche contra Wagner (1896), Götzendämmerung (1889) *and elsewhere are glossed over with characteristic glibness.*

First of all, Rosenberg attempted to relate Nietzsche to the German struggle of 1944.

... In this connection, and in view of the clash between two worlds, Nietzsche's position in *German* thinking and in *European* Being inspires us today in a unique fashion. I know how controversial these two elements were in his life, and that it is not difficult to bring to bear apparently contradictory, even mutually exclusive, quotations. However, when words drawn from totally different milieus and different epochs are placed next to one another, they become for us isolated, fleeting symbols, *particularly if we do not know the man and his total essence-structure.* Elements which can often be interpreted as indicating resistance or rejection, are often not indicative of a struggle against his own essence, against *Deutschtum*, but rather of a bitter

[4] 'Friedrich Nietzsche.'

clash with the world scene as it then appeared. Much of what appears to be hateful is, in essence, only wounded and disappointed love. Only if we understand this will we be able to grasp correctly the lives not only of Nietzsche but of so many fighters in Germany. I would like to recall only those beautiful words which represent the measure of Nietzsche's inner turmoil; here, he declared that he held so fervently to the pure and strong kernel of the German essence that he dared to expect it to reject those foreign elements that had been forcibly implanted within it; that he dared to expect that the German spirit would return to itself... 'Never believe that the German spirit has lost, for all eternity, its mythical homeland as long as it still comprehends the cries of the birds who speak of it. One day, it will awaken in the freshness of dawn, as if from a monstrous sleep. Then it will slay the dragon, annihilate the malicious dwarf and arouse Brünhilde—and then Wotan's spear itself will be unable to bar the way.'

*   *   *

After a discussion of Nietzsche's German nationalism, which Rosenberg says is shown by vestiges of anti-Semitism and anti-French feelings displayed while he was in the medical service during the Franco-Prussian War, he turns to Nietzsche's 'investigation' of the spiritual crisis that had beset the nineteenth century.

...He knew that the waters of religion had been stemmed and swamps and puddles left behind; that nations had separated as enemies and wanted to tear each other to pieces; and that the sciences were pushing on without any moderation and in blindest self-assurance. However, the cultured classes and states were borne along by a 'splendid, contemptible moneyed economy'. Never would the world be more mundane and poorer in love and kindness than during his time. The learned classes no longer represented either alms or refuge. Rather, they daily became more restless and less thoughtful and loving. Everything, including contemporary art and science, was contributing to the 'approaching barbarism'. The cultured proved to be the greatest enemies of culture, for they sought to prevaricate with regard to the general sickness, and they thus hindered any sort of cure. *Truth,* however, in regard to which this liberal, loveless society was preaching so much then, had become a completely undistinguished term for many, and the powers that be did not have to fear anything disorderly or out of the ordinary from it. According to Nietzsche, the 'truth' of the liberal age is a soothing and comfortable creature which would continuously support all established power and none should make any sort of fuss on its behalf. However, it would itself become a new centre of Inquisition, maintaining an absolute silence against any inconvenient phenomenon. It was therefore obvious that a certain gloom and mustiness weighed heavily upon the best people of the time – an eternal vexation over the battle between dissimulation and honesty, a battle which was waged in their own breasts. There was a lack of self-confidence, because one was incapable of being at the same time both a guide and a purveyor of culture for others. Knowledge, which once had raised itself so high in rebellion against other ages, had in many cases dethroned itself, and the spirit of a rootless journalism, which occasionally called itself philosophy, pressed upon the universities. With *Faust* and *Nathan the Wise* on his lips, 'the language and insights of

our nauseating literary journals', a smooth and clever
variety of lecturer attained the podium. Nietzsche was
against this: if one speaks of thinkers and of philosophers,
it is necessary for a philosopher to have an 'unbowing and
rough masculinity' about him. In this age, however, this
man had dropped out of sight and was to be found very
rarely. This ever declining course of events provided an
environment from whose inadequacies, as well as from
their own delicate natures, Hölderlin and Kleist would
have perished; they would not have been able to endure
the climate of this so-called German culture. Only
'strong natures, such as Beethoven, Goethe, Schopenhauer
and Wagner could endure'. Even such lonely figures,
however, needed love and needed companions before
whom they could be as open as if they were by themselves
and simply be themselves; a companion in whose presence
the cramp of silence and pretence was eased. If this
companion were taken away, one nurtured a growing
despair for the development of the German spirit. It
would be the worst possible action that one could take
against unusual men, to drive them so deeply into themselves that they would emerge in volcanic eruptions.
'Yet, there is always that demi-god who endures living,
and who lives victoriously under such terrible conditions —
if you want to hear his solitary song, listen to the music of
Beethoven.' In another place, Nietzsche declaims, 'How
is a great, productive spirit to find itself among a people
which is no longer certain of internal unity, with its
educated strata badly educated and inwardly sub-
verted? ... How can this spirit endure if the unity of
Volk-perception has passed; if he knows also that that
portion which calls itself the cultured part of the *Volk*
and which has appropriated to itself the artistic spirit

of the nation, falsifies and colours this perception?'

... Even in view of this total evaluation, Nietzsche hopes once more for a strong German heart, for a *German* form of scepticism, for 'the elevated spirit of Frederick the Great among intellectuals' and, more than once, he declared that today, when the animal herd alone was both honoured and bestowed honour in Europe; that in this Europe a totally different human type had to attain mastery in order to alter fate. He offered a thorough critique of the whole social structure, a critique of the Marxist movement, which at that time had already been falsely dubbed socialist—a critique which, in logic and devastation, is unthinkable even today. For him, Marxism is the tyranny of the least and the dumbest, i.e. of the superfluous, the envious and the hack-actor, carried to its final conclusion. It was in fact the ultimate consequence of 'modern ideas' and their latest anarchy. Nietzsche, above all, opposed the attempt to overthrow the property concept, because the overthrow of the property concept would encourage a destructive struggle for existence ...

It is understandable that thoughts of this nature—which were first put down in reasoned form and later on as aphorisms—when placed in the self-satisfied context of the liberal world, were ignored or murdered with laughter. The men of his time took no cognizance of them, even when Nietzsche prophetically depicted the complete hypocrisy of that paradise described in the Marxist programme, of the stateless ideal society in which class struggle did not exist.

'*Marxism requires a total subjugation of all citizens before an unconditional state, the like of which has never before existed.*' The premonition of that Marxist dictatorship which we see marching against us from Moscow as our mortal

enemy is clearly described here. It has allied itself with
those forces which Nietzsche had depicted as being
particularly dangerous. We cannot say that Nietzsche
could have perceived the entire structure and psychology
of the East in all its details. Nietzsche knew, however,
that in spite of all knowledge, the path of development
embarked upon probably could not be reversed within a
short period of time; that the great crisis of Germany and
the entire European continent had to result from this
mixture of liberalism, plutocracy and anarchy. He was
deeply convinced that this mish-mash introduced by the
entire liberal movement—and here he showed an in-
exhaustible hatred of Rousseau as the spiritual author
of the feuds—had to lead to the most fearful altercation
and perhaps also to tyranny. He believed that 'The
democratization of Europe is, at the same time, an involun-
tary arrangement for the nurturing of tyrants—this word
is to be understood in every sense, including the spiritual.'

This clear understanding of the most extreme of
developmental possibilities sets Nietzsche apart even more
clearly—as a thinker and as an active, militant philosopher
—from all the movements of his time. Nietzsche's discovery of the artistic confusion of style and his clear
recognition of the rootless present which encouraged
all varieties of self-contradicting traditions combined in
him to constitute a critique of his whole age; and a sharper
or more caustic one cannot be imagined.

*   *   *

According to Rosenberg, Nietzsche's spiritual collapse was
reflected in his change of attitude towards Wagner. It was also
symptomatic of an age which offered scant sympathy to one who

challenged its values. This unsympathetic attitude was a Europe-wide phenomenon. Germany alone was not to blame for Nietzsche's spiritual death.

... Even if, in many fields, one prophet or another of our time stands somewhat closer to us, Friedrich Nietzsche as a total personality and as an imperturbable observer of an entire epoch fated to collapse, was certainly the *greatest figure of the German and European intellectual world of his day*! With regard to all of his later avowals and critiques, we must conclude that he was wounded when-ever he made an utterance; and then he turned upon the immediate inflictor of the wound. This would have happened in the same way, whether he had lived in France, England or any other state. For everywhere the same phenomenon of decline was at work, destroying established traditions without being able to create new ones or to construct new ideals ...

*   *   *

Germany had inherited Nietzsche's heartfelt mission of saving Europe. The hard-pressed German armies were not merely defending Germany, but all of Western civilization.

The European *Kulturbürger*, his powers of resistance sapped by somnolence, is being overwhelmed by a once-dammed destructive fanaticism from the East; a fanatic-ism which, notably in alliance with Jewish-Western Marxism, has shaken not only Germany but the entire European continent, to its foundations. If, therefore, we are proud that National Socialist Germany alone still defends this old Europe today, we can proclaim, somewhat differently from Nietzsche in the nineteenth century, that today *we* are the 'good Europeans' [*sic*], for this is a right for which we have struggled honourably. At the same time, however, in order that we do not fall into that Tartuffery so rightly condemned by Nietzsche, we must humbly admit that many phenomena of the old age can still be detected among us; that many petit-bourgeois are still living in that musty atmosphere in which Nietzsche suffered so badly; that there is much limited, schematic thinking that has as yet not attained that freedom of which Nietzsche dreamed and about which we ourselves dream; and that many people are in danger of running around like Philistines instead of being like Faust. But, in spite of these perceptions, we still feel in our experience the great course of a new age; and we know that that which has borne us, and which has given the German nation of today the inner will for unyielding resistance, is also accounted for in the deep emotion of the lonely Nietzsche — emotion which carried him through a painful life in which loneliness often led to despair and accusation. At the same time, however, his life was always drawn forward by the unconditional necessity of this confrontation with the future ...

Thus, we National Socialists see today the effects which those powers — stemming from the past — began to develop in the nineteenth century: a dangerous, destructive strength whose great festering development has led to a fearful sickening of the European essence. And at the same time we see several prophets in the midst of these unhealthy streams, prophets compelled to raise their voices to smash these values which were so inimical to creativity, and to help develop a new life order.

Today, we honour the lonely Friedrich Nietzsche as one of them. After we strip away all that is time-bound and also all that is all-too-human, this figure today stands next

to us spiritually, and, reaching back in time, we greet
him as a near relation, as a spiritual brother in the
struggle for the rebirth of a greater German spirituality
and for the formation of broad-minded and all-inclusive
thought. We greet him as the proclaimer of that European
unity which is indispensable to the creative life of our old
continent, a continent which is today being rejuvenated
in a great revolution.

*   *   *

Naturally, like any good Kulturmensch, *Rosenberg had to
consider Goethe and how he represented that German creative
spirit which embraced Meister Eckhart, Leonardo da Vinci,
Michelangelo, Beethoven, Nietzsche, etc. In Goethe, Rosenberg
sees the ideal Nordic balance between activity and discipline.
He sums up by placing Goethe in the context of Nordic* Kultur.
The following is taken from Der Mythus des 20. Jahrhunderts.

Goethe could not do enough to draw attention tirelessly
to revivifying action, even to humble hard work, in
continuously new forms. The greatest hymn to human
activity is *Faust*. After circumnavigating and pressing
through all knowledge, all love and suffering, Faust is
freed through action. For that spirit which always strives
for infinity, a limited act, the damming of a flood in the
service of men, was the capstone of life, the last step
towards the unknown. The nobility of action is apotheosized in the work of art. 'The doctrine of true activity
shuts off the senses; for when words are lacking, action
speaks.' 'He who learns early of determinism will attain
freedom in comfort.' 'A man can only declare himself
free if he feels himself determined in the moment; if he
dares to declare himself as determined, he will feel

himself to be free.' 'A master is one who perceives that limitation, even for the greatest spirit, represents a necessary step towards the highest unfolding.' 'How can a man know himself: never through observation; most certainly, however, through activity. Attempt to do thy duty and thou wilt know what thou art. Duty, however, is the requirement of the day ... '

When Goethe had satiated all his senses in Rome, he wrote, 'I do not want to know how to do anything other than produce something and to utilize my senses correctly.' However, he also said, 'A new epoch is beginning for me. My mind has been so enlarged by all the many sights and perceptions that I must limit myself in manner of work.' Elsewhere, he summarizes thus, 'My life is observing and writing poetry. I have proceeded in a synthetic and analytical manner; the systole and diastole of the human spirit was a second wind for me.' When Schiller died he said, in order to muster his strength, 'Whenever I feel myself weakened, I look about for different activities'; and in 1823, when he was plagued by heavy spiritual and bodily burdens — when he had lost his son — he needed precisely that sanity which appeared to have abandoned him at the time. So he wrote, 'And now, forward over the graves.'

This spiritual condition of Goethe corresponds in essence to the active lives of all great men of the Nordic West. It can be seen in Leonardo's paintings of St Anne, the eyes of John the Baptist and the face of Christ, where he gives expression to an intangible, super-sensuous world. At the same time, he was an engineer, a lucid technician, who would not do enough to make even nature mechanically useful. One could say that a good number of Leonardo's maxims sprang from the mouth of Goethe. Beethoven, after deep, musical remoteness, suddenly moves to a cheerful scherzo, and the most gripping song of seclusion is the symphony of joy. Beethoven seemed to have been inspired by his dreams; however, at the same time he expressed the words of the dynamic Westerner, 'Strength is the credo of those who distinguish themselves before all others; it is also mine.' 'To grab fate by the throat' was posited as his goal. Michelangelo's personality was also made up from this same forceful mixture: we read his sonnets to Vittoria Colonna and then stand before his Sibyls and his Christ, damning the world. Also, it becomes clear to us that the Western mystique does not preclude life but that, on the contrary, it has selected the creative being itself as its partner. In order to elevate itself, it needs it as opposition; the more heroic the soul, the mightier will be its external works; the more secluded the personality, the more radiant will be the deed.

*   *   *

Rosenberg saw the Nordic creative spirit threatened by the growth of the Jew-dominated city. In the twentieth century, a degenerate art, symptomatic of atomized man, had arisen as an implied challenge to the strength of soul as represented by Michelangelo, Goethe, Rembrandt, Beethoven and Wagner. The following extract is taken from Mythus.

... The metropolis began its race-annihilating work. The coffee-houses of the asphalt men became studios; theoretical bastardized dialectics became laws for ever-new 'directions'. A race-chaos of Germans, Jews and anti-natural street races was abroad. The result was mongrel 'art'.

Vincent van Gogh, a man full of longing, but broken, went out to paint. At home at Schoole, he wanted his study of 'peasant figures at work' to be truly modern; the 'heart of modern art; something that neither the Renaissance, nor the Dutch school nor the Greeks have done'. He tortured himself with this idea, and confessed that if he had had the strength earlier he would have painted 'saintly figures'; they would have been men like the first Christians. 'Later', he would yet have the strength. As for now, he would be destroyed by the following thoughts: 'Just paint; don't think. Paint coal, lettuce, whatever it might be, to soothe yourself.' And Vincent painted apple trees, coal and cobblestones. Until he went mad. Gauguin sought his ideal in the South Seas. He depicted the race to which his black-skinned girlfriends belonged, melancholy nature, colourful leaves and ocean. Also, he was as inwardly brittle and torn as all those who searched the whole world for a long-lost beauty, whether they be named Böcklin, Feuerbach, Van Gogh or Gauguin. Until this type tired of the search and surrendered itself to chaos.

Once, Picasso copied the old masters with great care, while meantime painting strong images (one of these hangs with Schtschukin in Moscow) in order to be able finally to commend to an aimless public his theoretical illustrations in bright-dark squares as new art. The literary parasites greedily searched for the newest sensation and chattered about a new epoch in art. However, what Picasso had shamefully hidden behind geometrical patterns came out openly and insolently after the war. Mongrelism claimed that its bastardized progeny, nurtured by spiritual syphilis and artistic infantilism, was able to represent 'expressions of the soul'. One should gaze long and hard upon something like Kokoschka's *Self Portrait*, in order to gain a halfway understanding of the monstrous inner-nature of this idiot-art. In a novel,

Hanns Heinz Ewers tells of a child who was talented in so unnatural a manner as to derive a special satisfaction from the illness of elephantiasis. Our contemporary 'European intelligentsia' finds itself in a similar position today; an intelligentsia which, through Jewish pens, worships the Kokoschkas, Chagalls, Pechsteins and so on as the leaders of future art. Wherever this form goes it bears the features of degeneration, as in the case of Schwalback, who already has dared to represent Jesus as flat-footed and bow-legged. Lovis Corinth displayed a certain robustness, yet even this butcher of the brush pales in comparison with the clay-corpse-coloured bastardizations of Syrian Berlin.

Impressionism, which originally was borne by strong, talented artists, became a battle-cry of decomposing intellectualism. An atomistic world-view atomized even the colours; the dull level of understanding of natural science achieved its apogee in the practitioners and theoreticians of Impressionism. A mythless world pro-created a mythless sensousness. Men who desired inwardly to break free from this were broken. Van Gogh is a tragic example of one who longed and went mad. Gauguin is another example of the attempt to break free from intel-lectualism. Only the Paul Signacs painted on, uninhibited, unconcernedly, gluing their bits of colour next to one another.

These men stood helplessly in the present. Likewise, their opponents stood unsuspectingly with their backs to the future. Homeric fate which, it is said, Böcklin once accepted, had decided already. Today, too, it has become an inner impossibility to hang an 'Island of the Dead' upon the wall.

... The complete tragedy of a mythless age also revealed itself in the following decades. Men no longer wanted intellectualism; they began to hate the endless dissection of colour and to despise the brown gallery-colours and copies of Titian. With correct feeling, they began to search for redemption, expression and strength. And the result of this powerful tension was—the abortion of Expressionism. A whole race had cried for expression and now had nothing that it could express. It called for beauty and no longer had an ideal of beauty. It wanted to search for life in a revived spirit of creativity and it had lost every true ability to create form. Thus, Expressionism became a style: instead of nurturing a new style-constructing strength, it continued the process of atomization. Internally unprincipled they [the Expressionists] devoured 'primitive art', over-reached themselves in praise of Japan and China, and began in all seriousness to direct European-Nordic art back to Asia ... Thus, a bar-room mystique alternated with cerebralism and cubist linear chaos, until men became completely satiated and are today again searching, and in vain, with what they call 'New Realism'.

The essence of this completely chaotic development lies, among other places, in the loss of that beauty ideal which, while in many forms and costumes, still has remained the underlying support for all European creative art. Democratic, race-corrupting precepts and the *Volk*-annihilating metropolis combined with the carefully planned decomposing activities of the Jews. The result was not only the shattering of *Weltanschauung* and state thought, but also of the art of the Nordic West ...

*   *   *

The creative will of the Nordic Volk-*soul was under attack!*

How could the attack be met? Obviously, by revivifying Volk *art and thereby ending that atomization of soul which was a product of the insidious influences of Orientalism. In a series of articles Rosenberg gave concrete suggestions as to how German art must be reorientated. The first article given is from the November 1925 issue of* Der Weltkampf, *and provides a general description of what Rosenberg felt to be the situation of German art after the First World War, and the essence and goal of* Volk *art. The second article appeared earlier. in the May 10th, 1922 issue of the* Völkischer Beobachter, *and it constitutes a critique of some of the reactionary elements in* Volk *art. The third article appeared in July 1933, and was directed against those in the National Socialist movement who wanted to include elements of German Expressionism in the Nazi revolution. These first essays are taken from* Blut und Ehre ein Kampf für deutsche Wiedergeburt.

ON THE CURRENT ART STRUGGLE

If an age or a people no longer has a unified ideology, then it also no longer has an *art*. Isolated artists could exist in such an age, but a *style* is something that results from a general direction of soul. Therefore, we see today that we are also confronted with chaos in the field of art.

The end of the eighteenth century saw the *Sturm und Drang* in opposition to the classical ideal. The efforts of this group were brushed aside by the defenders of Hellenism, who sought to attain a formal aesthetic. The *Stürmer* and *Romantiker* Goethe became the author of the second *Faust*, while the revolutionary Schiller yielded the poet, 'approximating antic form'.

The perception and creativity of the West is dynamic, while the Greek ideal springs from a chiefly static constitution of soul. In Europe, rest was conceived of as the transitional step from movement to movement while Hellas desired to transform even the quickest motion into rest. The essence of Greece subsists in a self-supporting plastic art, while the essence of the West manifests itself in the most fluid architecture, in elusive painting and in explosive music. Greece was form, the West was forming, i.e. endless activity. Greece was predominantly plastic representation of body, while the West struggled towards the representation of soul.

When the machine age posed new problems of form, it became obvious that the West no longer possessed artists, but only art professors, archaeologists and grammarians on the one hand, and dull, often instinct-less, engineers, eclectics and mathematicians on the other.

To speak first of architecture: construction began of monstrous railroad stations, factories, warehouses with gushing Greek capitals, acanthus leaves, imitations of Moorish, Gothic and Chinese forms combined with the most crude iron-work. All of Europe is still overflowing with this evidence of an unparalleled artistic decline. And when a new generation sought to become 'personal', there arose the notorious Jugendstil, whose crimes of industrial art can be gazed upon from Paris to Moscow and Budapest. Even today, this rages unchecked in many places.

Creative strength was broken because it had orientated itself, ideologically and artistically, towards a foreign standard and thus was no longer attuned to the demands of life. Also, in nineteenth-century painting we see the classical schools suddenly turning towards subjectivism and finally ending up in the art-Bolshevism of today. If, at an earlier time, one wanted to represent only 'Greece', then 'Nature', today one wants to strike out the object altogether and represent 'spiritual experience' without form. We find parallel phenomena in music, poetry and the theatre as well.

Art and artist are fragmented. Thousands of people in all camps feel this. They are searching for a new unity, a new style, a new ideal of beauty; all of them, insofar as they are true. However, after the destruction of the classical standard, the bastardization of a Schönberg, of a Kokoschka, of a Becher triumphed over our still aimless artists, who have thrown off the old, but have yet to find the true, the new. A later age will prove whether the powers of *Volk* and race were strong enough to create a synthesis out of chaos.

Today, architecture is the first art which is on its way to being made honourable once again. They [the architects] are awaiting the mission of overthrowing the technical through technique and new creativity. Anyone who has eyes can see the self-conscious striving to create a true form which embodies the new dynamic of our life. We see this in the corn siloes of California, in a steamer of the North-German-Lloyd line, in the train station at Helsing-fors, on the bridges of Tauernbahn. There will come a time when this new search for truth will produce theatres, town halls and religious structures. Pityingly, and with shame, a modern architect gazes upon the Friedrichstrasse in Berlin, upon the Munich town hall and upon thousands of other signs of an inwardly false art and of ideological chaos.

In other arts, the struggle is raging still and it even appears as if the lowest level has not as yet been attained.

If one wants to speak of the principles of the coming art, he cannot speak of rules and credos, but only of a new spiritual direction. The *Volkish Weltanschauung* and method

of historical observation necessarily bring with them a
new truthfulness, one which discards the old compulsory
principles and shatters rotten veneers. Instinctively and
consciously, it discards the foreign and inimical—the
most important precondition for positive action. However,
it also brings with it an old, yet new, beauty ideal. It is old
in that it is in keeping with those racial values depicted
by the great Venetians (Titian, Palma Vecchio, Giorgione)
and represented by Raphael, Botticelli, Holbein, Dürer
and Van Eyck. It is old in that it was revived in Wagner's
creation. It is new in that it will be ensconced in the
strengths and form of the present.

Today we have no great poets because 'we' are not
yet ourselves. The World War has not brought them
forth because no one has yet attained the inner realization
that he fought and died for a new *Mythus*. Today, millions
of all nations ponder before the grave of the Unknown
Soldier; millions of Germans gaze upon grim tombs of
war. A short time ago, a plan was outlined in which a holy
wood would be erected to the memory of the heroes of the
World War. *Soon, we will realize that these twelve million
men of the white race are martyrs; that all of them are both
sacrificial victims of a collapsed age and heralds of a new one.
They, the dead of today, are the living links between millions of
individuals, the founders of the* Volkish *Mythus. They are the
most sublime witnesses to the eternity of race and* Volk.
*Once this is realized, the poets of the World War will be born.
However, a new* Kultur *and a new art will one day also be
able to develop from this* Mythus.

This mythical experience is the foundation, the singular
foundation of our future. It is this alone which makes a
life and art style possible. The past created church and
court styles, it gave us a Hellenic or Roman unity. The

task of the present is to prepare a *Volkish* racial unity — or
to sink into civilized barbarism.

VOLKISH ART

The *Volkish* movement correctly designates itself as a
spiritual as well as a political current, one which has
broken with collapsed forms of state-thought and many
given forms of life and art; a movement which seeks to
blaze new trails for everything that is alive and progressive.
Politically, *Volkish* thinking has preserved its clear imprint
in National Socialism, and under its banner active Germans are currently fighting for a new state-thought.
However, it is curious that if we observe what one likes to
call *Volkish* art, little of this elementary pressing forward
is to be seen.

If one speaks of the state-thought of the Middle Ages,
of Frederick the Great, of the French kings and of liberal
democracy, we are speaking of a *past* which, to be sure,
contributed one element or another to the foundation of
the new construction of the future; however, none of these
patterns of thought has become a compulsory political
principle for us.

When we first turn our attention to painting we see,
in contrast, this distressing phenomenon: the majority
of our *Volkish* painters gaze as if transfixed only upon the
art of the past. Naturally, we must admit that many of
our present artists view the world through eyes similar
to those of a Schongauer and a Ludwig Richter.[5] However,

[5] Martin Schongauer (c. 1450–93) was an Alsatian painter noted for
forceful realism in oil painting. He was an influence upon Dürer and Holbein.
Ludwig Richter (1803–44), was a well-known illustrator of fairy-tale books.
He also painted rather plain domestic scenes and German landscapes. He is
often singled out as being indicative of the 'Biedermeyer' approach to
aesthetics. (Ed.)

it is curious that the present *Volkish* artist believes that he must emphasize, in abundant imitation, the old form of his *Volkish* art. Thus, the representatives of this school have no understanding at all of present pressures, and all too often we see coming from them a fundamental denial of the collective, germinating strengths of the present. They are doing the same thing that in the field of politics the conservatives have done *vis-à-vis* the worker movement. Instead of listening with sensitive ear to the rhythm of the present, people surrounded themselves with books and pictures of past epochs, and were then irritated and bewildered when chaotic movements suddenly became visible everywhere. As in the area of politics, where a well-justified workers' movement could be falsified through Jewish Marxism because old national leaders were petrified in the conservative camp, an age's longing for new art-forms has been betrayed in the area of art.

Instead of empathizing with the unavoidable inner break with the past and making possible an organic development of the new, vital strengths which appear in storm and stress, many of our mature *Volkish* artists have eschewed this new longing and have handed over to an entire generation a power which misuses and falsifies the new longing of today. It doesn't do to break one's staff in Pharisaical arrogance over the whole new age. Rather, we must disengage ourselves from those clever souls who, through a poisoning of their spiritual well-springs, have become untrue to themselves. The present time has more of a right to demand expression than have the crack-pots and groaners over a dead artistic past. Only an artist who understands the drives of the present will also be able to find the relevant artistic form. Here, naturally, art—as other fields—cannot be helped by theoretical considerations, but solely by *experience*. To look and prepare for it is the duty of every German.

REVOLUTION IN THE FINE ARTS?

First of all, the political revolution of National Socialism is the most important step of the movement. This is true, however, only because it signifies the externalization of a *socialist-spiritual* revolution in the German people. The great uprising is not self-contained, but rather is directed towards certain goals, driven by certain wills. Therefore, ever-new areas of life are engulfed by the coursing waves of the movement, and millions of souls are excited anew and spurred on towards organization.

The fine arts have also engaged in bitter clashes of opinion for a long time, and it is completely understandable that *politically* like-minded National Socialists have quite differing opinions when it comes to art and — even with regard to passing judgment on certain artists — often engage in lively controversy.

We can all agree that the mendacious pseudo-baroque of the nineteenth century was just as unbearable as the 'engineer art' of today. In judging the helpless protest against this, the Jugendstil, one opinion predominates. All National Socialists are certainly of one mind with regard to that great exhibition of men's fashion over the centuries called the Siegesallee. However, a temperamental clash has broken out over such men as Nolde and Barlach. One group of Nationalist Socialist artists wants to exclude them from the ideological bases of the coming art, while another group, which calls itself *revolutionary*, bears them on its shield.

If we attempt to rise above all subjectivity and arrive at a judgment which conforms with the *collective* thought of National Socialism, we will have to ascertain that in spite of all differences in fashion and dress, in spite of the passage of a thousand years, in spite of every political upheaval, the Northern artist has been dominated by a well-defined beauty ideal. Nowhere does this powerful nature-related idea strike us more beautifully than in Greece. However, it dominates in Titian as well; also in Palma Vecchio, Giorgione and Botticelli, who painted 'Gretchenish' figures. This ideal comes to light in Holbein also, as in his painting of Gudrung, and in Goethe's *Hermann und Dorothea*. It stands out in the face of Pericles as well as in that of the Bamberger trooper.

It doesn't matter whether a given *individual* now corresponds completely to the ideal, as long as a *longing* for that ideal is alive, the nation is in proximity to it and united in nature. It is this *intuitive quality* which, binding itself with figure and form, prepares the way to the future in the field of painting and the plastic arts. If, on the basis of *this* viewpoint, one now asks what our attitude towards Nolde and Barlach must be, we will be able, or I at least believe that I am able to say, that there can be little doubt that both artists display an outspoken talent. For example, a Nolde seascape which hangs in the Crown Prince's palace, is strongly and forcefully painted. However, other representative attempts are negroid, irreverent, raw and devoid of true inner strength of form. On this side, Barlach dominates his materials like a virtuoso, and no one will deny the monumentality of his woodcuts. But whenever he represents men, he is *foreign*, completely foreign. We see earth-round temperance and a *joy* in the burdensome heaviness of materials. These are no 'Mecklenburg Farmers'. Oh no, the latter stride over the field in a *completely different* way to those figures of

Barlach's humanity! And finally, we gaze upon Barlach's Magdeburg War Memorial, which was completed for the church there: little, half-idiotic admixtures of undefinable human types with Soviet helmets are supposed to represent German fighting men! I believe that *any* healthy SA man could here arrive at the same judgment as a conscious artist. *I*, in any case, have found men like the Noldes and the Barlachs to be self-inspired 'revolutionaries', most of whom have little real contact with the fine arts, but who now believe that they also must be active in this area.

By the way, it is no accident that Nolde and Barlach were so spiritedly pushed into the foreground by the November gentlemen,[6] people who openly thundered that the work of both artists was an aberration of German art; similar to Otto Braun, who was an aberration of German politics.[7]

Without further ado, we will welcome a painter or sculptor, who, while not yet working for the movement, has a thoroughly great style, and offers a sincere interpretation. We should wait modestly for him and then readily admit him. But we should not compulsively put upon pedestals painters who have already outlived their usefulness simply in order to have reserves against reaction. These troops are *inwardly not authentic* — and *this* is decisive.

These explanations should in no way be interpreted as neutralizing a *forward* drive; on the contrary! An old world is gone for ever. As I was careful to point out six years ago, a romanticism of *steel* has taken the place of one of dreams. This longing is alive and groping for form in

[6] A derogatory term for those who established the Weimar Republic. (Ed.)
[7] Otto Braun was a prominent Social Democrat who played an important role in the Prussian government between 1919 and 1932. (Ed.)

millions of people. It doesn't upset anything if different paths are sought out. However, for every true National Socialist this search lies beyond the borders of political definition. How the German landscape is to be felt; how the heroic figure of the German warrior appears to be forged—these are the areas in which instinct and judgments of taste should test themselves. Then the outcome of this struggle will determine the form and content-world of our future.

*   *   *

In a speech on June 7th, 1935, Rosenberg consummated his (and Hitler's) victory over attempts to include Expressionism in the Nazi Revolution. The following speech, 'Weltanschauung und Kunst' is taken from Gestaltung der Idee, Blut und Ehre *II. Band, herausgegeben von Thilo von Trotha, (München, 1936).*

... therefore it is a new and yet old attempt to alter the relationships between personality, *Volk* and state, and, in this attempt, the *concept of freedom* is once more placed in the centre of thought. Freedom, as seen from the viewpoint of National Socialist thought, is not to be understood as unchecked individualism, but as a creative achievement of the individual being, as a representation of his inner strength, and also as a representation of that blood and character which provide the *preconditions* for this personality. Therefore, we do not conceive of the individual being as an isolated phenomenon, but, above all, as the healthy essence of *Volkstum*.

And when we bring together a National Socialist *Kulturgemeinde*,[8] we want to express immediately that we

[8] Literally culture-community, the major National Socialist culture organization. (Ed.)

consider it the highest duty of National Socialist *Weltan-schauung* to create a unity between personality, *Volk* and state by collecting all those strengths which — from a common will for new life values and a new life form — can promote every expression of artistic creativity which expresses what millions feel, and that which endows artistic style upon the unformed, yet living feelings of millions of human hearts.

There arises from the idea of *Kulturgemeinde* the duty to *nurture* culture. Biologically as well as spiritually understood, this means that we have the duty above all to promote organic growth, to promote that which is inwardly strong and necessary to life, that which serves the values of Germans and their beauty ideal. At the same time, the *Gemeinde* must keep as far away as possible any growth which is sick or inwardly foreign, and which does not act in the best interests of *Deutschtum* but in the interest of undermining the German being.

*   *   *

Rosenberg then goes on to repeat earlier attacks upon those National Socialists sympathetic to 'degenerate art'.

... this year, a mighty polemic has raged over many of these artists. I do not feel that it is necessary to list their names here, but we stand before the issue of whether National Socialism — which arose as a movement of German pride and self-respect — should foster *an art whose content and form contradicts to the letter all the values which have borne the National Socialist movement and which led to its victory.* In this regard, we do not want to suppress these artists politically; we will cheerfully leave alone all those

who enjoy them. However, here and now—and completely openly—we forbid these men for all time to talk
themselves into being standard-bearers of National
Socialist revolutionary art. We hope that the great
National Socialist movement will become ever more
conscious of the necessity of this clear position, and will
always stand against any such attempt, no matter whence
it comes. The National Socialist movement, therefore, will
always have to prohibit men who have had nothing to do
with this great movement of struggle, have not participated in it, or even spiritually *opposed* it, from becoming
its spokesmen. That art which we are convinced is and
will remain foreign to our entire being—even though it
might be dubbed with the honourable phrase National
Socialist—must be forbidden by the movement; and what
we, and not what others say, is decisive. Therefore, we are
convinced that it is the duty of our gallery directors not to
watch out for words of the past and to treasure them in all
their aspects, but to be attentive to what is developing
in German strength *today*—even if this has been scorned
or suppressed for decades, and even if this manifests itself
as an *immature* strength.

This year, we have consciously fought against *Jewish
domination* in all fields of culture as well as in the field of
politics, and we know only too well that Judaism has been
responsible for the most fearful poisoning in the area of
culture. The purposes of these efforts would be defeated
if, in a roundabout way, Jews under pseudonyms were
allowed to go back 'into business' again. We are also of the
opinion that artistic personalities who, in themselves, we
are ready to promote at any time, but who have gathered
the laurels of the November Republic, should no longer
have the right to influence the *art policy* of the National

Socialist movement for the purpose of allowing their old Jewish patrons to ensconce themselves once again in German artistic life as so-called 'good, exceptional Jews'.

As a total movement, we must once again harken to the words of the Führer in Nuremberg in the years 1933 and 1934, when he said that art is a sacred concern of the German people, that, as a revolutionary and ideological movement, we have the duty to advance it with all means, and that, therefore, the leaders of decay will never and *under no conditions* be able to be the standard-bearers of *our* time. For they have either lied previously or are lying today; in *both* cases the National Socialist movement does not see itself in the position of belonging to them ... In the field of *music*, Germany has always been not only a playground for 'interesting' and comprehensible experimentation, but also in the line of march of those powers who, in general, sought to tear out the roots of German melody and eternal German musical feeling. The whole *atonal* movement contradicts the rhythm of blood and soul of the German people, and *therefore* has been promoted by earlier political rulers, and a large number of partially gifted and less gifted musicians have placed themselves at the disposal of their plans. Beyond this, German music has gradually become a part of our daily life, and the great German musicians of the past speak to us today in exactly the same way as they did earlier.

*   *   *

The following two articles appeared in the November 1925 issue of Der Weltkampf. *They are taken from* Blut und Ehre ein Kampf für deutsche Wiedergeburt.

THE THEATRE

German art is an avowal of personality. Even in the theatre. The Greeks placed their actors upon a high stage, concealed them behind immovable masks and, through the use of a giant arena, shut out the personal, while creating so-called formal laws which later—when the pseudo-French tragedy dominated—stifled every true dramatic creative strength in Europe. (Moreover, Greek drama did not provide for any internal development. 'Fate' was an elemental, external catastrophe, not an inner occurrence bound up with the subject.) The Greek stripped his hero of personality; he 'harmonized', while the German characterized. He created figures, while the German created expression. The Hellene depicted the destruction or victory of the person; the German the guilt, victory and sin of spiritual personality.

The chains of foreign drama were broken by Molière and Shakespeare. Both produced their dramas in the midst of their respective milieus, without pseudo-classical trappings and laws. Shakespeare's entire art is a singular breakthrough within the pseudo-classical heritage. Lessing theoretically confirmed this adherence to law. However, in pursuit of a new pseudo-humanitarian ideal, he created the precondition for a much worse poison: the Jewish plague in today's theatre.

If someone had visited the Moscow Art Theatre before the war, he could have found a conception of true, dramatic art. Down to the last supernumerary, every participant contributed harmoniously to the entire work; all were artists through and through. Mastery of the material was naturally a precondition. Even prompting was rejected and applause forbidden. By virtue of this, every element that contributed to the appearance of theatre and which contributed to its abstract nature was cut out. This produced that artistic seriousness whch was once demanded by Schiller and Goethe; as a result, deep impressions were created of which none who visited this outwardly so untheatrical a theatre was ever deprived. No doubt, a deep Russian *Volk*-culture provided the source for the effects produced by the art of Stanislawski, Katschikow and by the decorator Robuschinsky. This drawing upon *Volkstum*, and the serious service to spiritual values which were born of it, provided the preconditions for the success of the theatre's artistic programme, one which was led by dilettantes. Naturally, this is due to the fact that the Russian is artistically gifted, particularly in the fields of theatre and dance. In Germany, we have had this experience: while several totally great artists have appeared, the general level of the players unfortunately leaves much to be desired. Consequently, the spectator has had to deal with too many abstractions, i.e. he is again and again compelled to overcome imbalances, a matter which is not his problem but rather that of the actors and directors.

When the West-European theatre fell into Jewish hands, its purely commercial management reached its summit. The pursuit of the 'star' is, even today, responsible for the inartistic essence of our theatre directors; it is a phenomenon which stipulates that everything else be trash. Moreover, if one fundamentally deprecates inwardness one continually seeks to impress through quantity. Reinhardt-Goldmann's performances of *Oedipus*, for example, reveal these efforts most clearly. The theatre became transformed into a mob, and art into mass-hypnosis and sensual excitement. In a similar way, Mahler's aspirations are revealed in his thousand-voiced orchestra. As a result of the breakthrough of the Jewish business spirit into the theatre, we have neither a French, nor a German nor a Jewish theatre, but a typical symptom of bastardization. The ability of Germans to depict heroes with particular clarity has become an abomination when placed in Jewish hands.

If one asks about fundamentals, we must be very clear about this — there is only one way open: the way, chosen in its time, by the Moscow Art Theatre. This theatre drew upon the past and present *Volkish* essence. It distilled dramatic essence from the theatre. This meant an overthrow of techniques by craft. All of this is possible only if that which is foreign is recognized as such. As Shakespeare overcame pseudo-Hellenic 'laws', so does the dramatist or director stand before a task of an opposite nature: the overthrow of dissolution and decadence in order to create a true *national theatre style*.

With regard to decoration, the quarrel is gradually being ironed out. Materialistic decoration is finally being overthrown. It confronted the spectator with too much, and finally, like most imitation, it left a trashy impression. The opposite swing of the pendulum had led to the stage of reform, and to a cold, anti-natural Expressionism. But even here it soon became plain that the expressionistic (Jewish-led) stage, which ostensibly was supposed to draw the spectator away from imitation, required a restoration of phantasy and, still more, restoration of the nonsensical elements which restrict dramatic experience. Both extremes sinned against the most essential requirements of scenery: 1. that it should not distract, and 2. that it should bother the observer with the least possible amount of abstraction. In view of our present age of decay, these requirements mean something which is almost impossible: the renunciation of effect. And yet, this is the first and the last condition for the rebirth of theatre.

Different attempts to bring back to life a truly national theatre have been undertaken. For economic reasons, they have all collapsed. As I see it (I admit that I am no theatre specialist), they emphasize their good, patriotic commitment, promise to put on only German pieces, demand only German actors and directors. At the same time, however, they still adhere to the old artistic programme stereotypes without noticing that we National Socialists are and must be not only political, but also cultural revolutionaries. The old nationalism was so bound up with economics and industry that it no longer bore any relationship to true *Volkish* thinking and feeling. It was completely barren of ideas, and stood helpless before a Jewish instinct-driven decay-activity. If the 'national' German industry understood what character-building (and -destroying) influences the theatre represents, and how necessary it is to revive continuously the *Volk* soul and to weld together common true experiences, we would have had a good theatre essence a long time ago. However, 'national' industry and our 'national' economy have, for so long, been the servant of Jewish high finance, that they dare less today than previously to cherish obvious *Volkish* art ideas. They have coal, paper, copper and potash on their minds, but no ideas of *Volkish Kultur*. Their hearts throb for dividends and not for struggling artistic creativity. The Jew banker patronizes his literary *Volk* and race comrades, allowing his newspapers to spread their fame. The German kings of industry, and the French and English ones also, unfortunately all too often view writers and actors as parasitical journeymen.

From Vienna, the *New Vienna Journal* of October 16th,

1925, a Jewish newspaper, radiating scorn and joy, reports:

> As we have learned, the project to construct an Aryan theatre in Vienna, in which only pieces of Aryan playwrights were to be performed by Aryan players before Aryan audiences, has collapsed completely. In order to have a somewhat secure basis for the proposed theatre-foundation, the attempt was made to form an Aryan theatre union, with a minimum membership of 15,000 persons—this to insure that there would be at least 500 assured theatre patrons per day. In spite of great propaganda, only a very few interested individuals could be found in Vienna and, for the present, the carrying out of this project has been abandoned.

The plundering of an entire people has succeeded almost effortlessly. It will be a long time until a political power struggle will create the prerequisites for *Volkish* cultural achievement. Until then, however, we ourselves must be clear about which ideas have caused the decay and which principles will guarantee a rebirth.

For this, we first of all do not require individual new thoughts as much as we do new thinking.

THE FILM

There has been much outcry over the film, particularly in *Volkish* circles. With some justice they refer to the monstrous flood of the most inferior films, and the degenerate criminal and moral film. From this awareness, there emerges a damning judgment. At one time, the printer's art was looked upon as an invention of Satan; it has often had satanic effects, and yet none of us would want to be without it. Nothing occurs in this life without a price ...

As in the case of the theatre, the question of film is a question of style. Without a doubt, the essence of the theatre signifies drama, i.e. spiritual depth, the inner link between man and fate, be it tragic or comic. The transference of this concept of style from the theatre to the film was the first source of that mistake which we entitle the 'kine-drama'. The theatre is three dimensional while the film is two dimensional. In the theatre, one externalizes that which is internal; in the film, we must begin with the image, i.e. take one's point of departure from the eye. It therefore contradicts style and is unjust to demand of this new means of representation something other than that which can be accomplished in its own style.

The first law of the film is this: not to set psychology in motion, but to speak through images. Only if one has decided to focus upon this two-dimensional activity can one hope to make a deep impression upon the spectator.

Beyond doubt, in the course of many years of experience German film producers have arrived at this new point of view. At the same time, however, they are concerned with widening the possibilities for film through incorporating those characteristics which, from time immemorial, have provided the bases for theatre. The play, in the truest sense of the word, and story-telling from sagas and the present have been revived by the film today, and it is these which exercise that great influence upon millions of people. To be sure, adventure and crime films have promoted much unwholesomeness. However, permit me to make the heretical observation that the film also has reopened, for millions of people, that source of phantasy which has been stopped up by the dirt of the great cities. Let us simply consider the present-day city minus the film: gigantic stone wastelands, dirty courtyards, grey walls, glittering lights and human restlessness. The theatre has become inaccessible to millions. Suddenly, there arises for these abandoned ones the possibility of travelling to distant lands, of experiencing adventure, of laughing over the grotesque and of weeping over 'feelings'. A whole world passes upon the screen and in the midst of an age of dead machinery, a new Romanticism has been born.

The darkened room allows each man to feel alone and unobserved; customary inhibitions fall away inside, forgotten phantasies are reawakened and the unwinding film is experienced as reality, indeed unconsciously as a medium which bears us away over time and space.

The cinema has become a substitute for millions of books. The present-day youth longing for adventure reads Karl May less and instead, sees Tom Mix in the cinema, and is enthralled by the powers of Marco. The young girl, thank God, reads Marlitt and Eschstruth and Heimburg less, and now instead has Henny Porten and Asta Nielson.[9] We needn't get excited over the silliness and sentimentality. They also are part of life, and there has never been an age, however great, in which man has not had to pay his tribute to the all-too-human.

Therefore, one should not discuss the film sanctimoniously (those who do this publicly, often sneak, willingly enough, to the movies); rather one should realize that through its discovery an implement has been placed in human hands which, if utilized by those conscious of goals, could cause millions of hearts to beat in a single direction.

[9] The first three names are those of sentimental novelists; the last two are actresses of the 1920s. (Ed.)

Today, a cinema industry has been spawned from the movie art and overwhelmingly this industry is found to be in the hands of the Jews. For this reason, the film has become a means of infecting the *Volk*—through lascivious images; and, just as clearly as in the Jewish press, there are revealed here plans for the glorification of crime. At the same time, all Europe is being overwhelmed by American productions which, grotesque as they are, provoke a unique variety of laughter, but, when viewed from another angle, are so hopelessly shallow, dumb and uncultured that in fact they constitute a great danger.

Many Scandinavian and German film directors have concerned themselves, in part successfully, with restoring the tarnished reputation of the film. Recently in Berlin, amidst cries of rage from Jewish film concerns, a patriotic enterprise has been undertaken. The censor in Marxist-misruled Prussia, who indecently passes every subversive film, forbade even the mere names of King Frederick William III and Blücher to appear in the titles. Here it is revealed that even in the round-about area of culture-politics, those inimical to Germany are attempting to hinder the rejuvenation of our *Volk*. Also revealed is the fact that all problems of today eventually end up as being problems of power. In most states, the thing has gone so far that the struggle against the great trusts can no longer be won by economic and artistic means alone. On this is based the unconditional demand: to support with every effort those political power-groups who, by providing *Volkish* phantasy in theatre and film with worthwhile material, elevate it and do not wish to poison and destroy it.

The practical means would be that all *Volkish* groups should decide on the construction of a model cinema.

These German undertakings must be assured support, in order that their artistic experiences may once again be placed in the service, in the deepest sense, of the national cause. Perhaps the suggestion offered here will not be completely fruitless. For example, in Budapest, 'Awakened Hungary' possesses three theatres, the income from which has made easier its work of *Volkish* enlightenment. With a good, artistic programme which is both national and varied, the right will can produce good results in Germany also—that is, the final, relentless excision of the Syrian-Jewish influence.

IV. THE ENEMY

The devil, the 'plastic demon', as Wagner had referred to him, was the Jew. Throughout his writings, Rosenberg systematically depersonalized the Jew into being a soulless creature, while, at the same time, personalizing *him to the extent that every German could identify the Jews with everything personally revolting. Intellectual anti-Semitism had a well-established pedigree in Germany. Luther, Fichte, Wagner, Schopenhauer, Treitschke — all had espoused anti-Semitism with varying degrees of virulence and commitment. Perhaps not the* logical culmination, *but certainly a* culmination of this *well-documented tradition was attained in Rosenberg's writings. The following selections are taken from* Die Spur des Juden im Wandel der Zeiten. *But similar opinions can be found throughout Rosenberg's writings.*

The great lie which we have been constantly spoon-fed is that the Jews, through dispersion and prejudicial laws, were shut out from all activities other than trade and were thus compelled to become moneylenders. Completely to the contrary: the Jew wandered about *because* he hoped to find in foreign lands the best areas for success. Thus it is no accident that the greatest centres of trade sprang up precisely where the most flourishing Jewish colonies existed; for if the Jewish heart had longed for work, he would have gone to lands with fruitful soil, and not to rocky islands and to the narrow quarters of port cities. We can find examples of this hoary phenomenon in pleasingly great numbers throughout all ages and lands.

For example, in the Basque land of Spain there were few cities, so with the idea of encouraging commerce and trade in these provinces, Sancho the Wise (1189) removed the old ordinances regarding visitors to the city and issued an edict which provided that every foreigner who sold goods could live in the city tax-free. As a result, a horde of Jews immediately came from all parts of Spain, in order not to pass up this splendid opportunity.* When, in Persia, Abbas Sophia wanted to revive economically his war-ravaged land, he guaranteed considerable privileges to foreign trading people. Here also, the result was that Jews, as well as other peoples, streamed in in great numbers from all regions.† The same thing happened in Poland, Bohemia and other states. The Jew had no feeling for a homeland, could not get such a feeling anywhere, did not yearn to do so, and therefore appeared as an eternal wanderer wherever the middleman-business or usury could prosper.

At the basis of this there lies a uniqueness of character which has become ever more fixed through the ages, and which cannot be lied away. However, it was not a character which was forced upon the Jews by evil men. While the Anglo-Saxon, the Scandinavian and the German travelled abroad in order to make vacant land usable, while they built their farms and their lives in foreign lands with plough in hand (and their race-brothers with different dispositions explored earth and the cosmos), the Jews flowed irresistibly towards the colourful turmoil of port cities, exchange offices and fairs ... In short, the Jews, throughout history, followed the classical Talmudic injunction—Traktat Jebamat, 66a ff:

* Kayserling, *Die Juden in Navarra*, p. 114.
† Schudt, *Jüdische Merkwürdigkeiten*, vol. 1, p. 27.

'If one makes 100 florins in trade, one can enjoy meat and wine daily; however 100 florins in farming barely yields salt and cabbage.' And when Rabbi Eleazer saw a field in which cabbage had been planted across its entire width, he said, 'Even if one wished to plant cabbage along its entire length, commerce is better than thou art.' Once, when the rabbi walked between ears of corn and observed how they swayed back and forth, he said, 'Thou canst sway for ever more; commerce is superior to thee.'

Usury and fraud were the order of the day from time immemorial; we keenly read the prophets who never grew tired of denouncing these peculiarities. Furthermore, the continual exhortations to honesty which are found in the Talmud, while indeed honouring the preachers, point out that they were not heard (besides, these exhortations concerned only the activities of Jews among themselves).

... If one reads travel descriptions from different ages, one meets this ever-recurring phenomenon: the inhabitants of all lands in which Jews are found in great numbers are surfeited with accusations of the deceitful trade of the Jews and their unbearable usury. And if the Jews and their hoodwinked friends are about to dismiss this as simple envy, they are indeed counting upon the childishness of the reader. If the phenomenon of Judaism everywhere calls forth these results, there must be another reason than jealousy of the inhabitants. But we do not have to take refuge in theoretical insights. For the most part, the facts from all ages are so reliable and numerous that one could open up any good book to gain support for this viewpoint, and then have to shield oneself from the quantity of evidence, rather than having to search for it.

* * *

As Rosenberg saw it, the evil influence of Jewish economic power attained a high point in the Middle Ages. Here he displayed great talent in being able to fuse elements of popular anti-Semitism with the more esoteric varieties of it rationalized in his own theories.

... If one reads reports on Jewish trade in the Middle Ages, as recorded by German chroniclers, we notice their continual astonishment over Jewish trickery. They recount the constant recurrence of falsification in exchange; feigned bankruptcy; the enticement of young inexperienced people—the children of rich parents—to wastefulness; promissory notes written in Hebrew and accepted in faith, notes which, when translated, turned out to contain nothing but an uncouth sentence; the switching of packages after purchase, so that the purchaser would find stones or straw instead of what he purchased. Often, a humorous note creeps into these accusations; for example, when the writer attempts to symbolize dramatically the relationship between Jew and Christian: 'A prince who places Jews among his subjects is doing the same as a housekeeper who fills a pond with young fish and then throws in a few large pike which devour the brood. Who is so foolish that he places a goat before a gardener? Who would want to make a fox guardian of geese or protector of chickens? Believe me, dear magistrates, if thou wouldst plague thy people, place Jews in thy lands.'*

* Jud, *Schlangenhaut*, pp. 3, 5, 80.

I would use up too much space if I were to investigate this more closely. It has been determined that in all times in all the lands in which Jews lived in great numbers, people raised the same accusation against Jewish deceit and Jewish usury.

With regard to these facts and to their indisputable justification, we have another and more important insight.

Naturally, unclean elements are to be found among Christians also, and there was certainly no lack of thieves and rogues. However, while all are united in their judgment against swindling, Jewish law draws an outspoken distinction between relationships between Jews and relationships between Jews and non-Jews.

No one today can have the slightest doubt that there was such a distinction, despite the natural efforts of the Jews to pose as those anointed with the oil of humanitarianism. They have succeeded in this also, for we have all shared the same error of regarding the Jewish element from the point of view of a German or Christian *Weltanschauung* and moral code, and we are thereby easily inclined to bring to bear thinking from which the Jews were far removed. For example, where we speak of neighbours, by it meaning each man, the Jew means only other Jews. Those commands one encounters in the Pentateuch, which sound so humane to us and which lie buried in the wilderness of the Talmud like oases and which we, taking them as something humane, are quite willing to accept—these commands preserve a bitter flavour through repeated differentiation between Jews and Goyim (non-Jews, heathen).

In the Traktat Baba Kamma 113b ff, we read: 'In

Deut. 22:3, where it speaks of things lost by your brother, it means: thou shalt return it to thy brother; however, thou shalt not return it to a heathen.' Rabbi Chaupina has said; 'What does it mean when it says, in Lev. 25:17, "Thou shalt not take advantage of thine neighbour?" Answer. Thou shalt not harm one to whom thou art bound in Torah and scriptures.'* In other places it is taught that the prohibition against stealing concerns only Jews in relationship to one another, and that even this is limited to kidnapping.†

The conversation between Jacob and Rachael, which is written down in the Talmud, can be called a classic. Jacob said to Rachael, 'Wilt thou marry me?' She answered, 'Yes, certainly, but my father is a deceiver and thou canst not get to him.' Jacob said, 'I am his brother in deceit.' Then she asked, 'Is it permitted that a just man be great in deceit?' Jacob said, 'Show thyself pure to the pure and trustless to the false. See Psalms 18, 27.' ‡

When we ... attack the Jews, this is not done in order to deprecate freedom of thought—as they, with feigned shock, claim—but in order to sustain an attack on a legal view which runs completely counter to all states. Once and for all, it must be ascertained that a race which has this view of law is not capable of being judged by Europeans, and that consequently public offices must be shielded from Jewish influence. For a Jewish judge would have to act in general to protect and defend only Jews.

Those who naively indulge in humaneness now say that Jewish laws no longer apply in our prosperous age. Op-

---

* Baba Mezia, 39a ff.
† Sanhedrin, 86a ff.
‡ Traktat Megilla, 12a ff.

posed to this is the fact that approximately nine million Jews, i.e. almost two-thirds of the Jews of the world, are still the strongest of adherents to the Talmud. Because of this, the laws of all states have been, from time immemorial, a thorn in the side of the Jews, and they have attempted to act against them or, with Talmudic cleverness, to interpret them for their own purposes. Thus, we can also see that the Jews have seldom troubled themselves with attaining equality, as citizens in all professions, but rather, have attempted to free themselves from taxation and have fought for special conditions and special laws ... To be sure, the laws of state somewhat mechanically hindered, the Jews in this practice. However, whenever this ban was loosened — by whatever variety of influence — then the Jew immediately and energetically plunged into the breach. We see it today in Russia and, until 1933, we saw it in Germany. It makes no difference to say that the big-city Jew had nothing to do with the laws of the Talmud. For the Talmud did not make the Jews; rather the Jews made the Talmud. Besides, this book has already dominated Jewish spiritual life for two thousand years; it is crammed into children every day from the age of six. Therefore, it has naturally developed further the character of all Jews in a given direction, whether they are atheistic Bourse-speculators, religious fanatics or Talmudic Jews of the cloth. Furthermore, many of our big-city Jews stem, fairly directly, from little villages in Galicia and Poland ...

*   *   *

Rosenberg focused upon Jewish exclusiveness, and the 'intolerance' which such a feeling necessitated.

If the Jew is consciously divorced from other peoples in moral, legal and national questions, it is natural that his religious thinking was no exception. If his people was chosen, he generally considered his religion to be the only valid one.

Jahweh, whose efficacy had been limited in ancient times to the territory of Canaan, grew and grew and, in the imagination of the Jews, He took the shape of a Godhead, becoming ever-mightier and all-embracing. However, this did not preclude His being worshipped as a national God, who protected and led Israel in that capacity. The high walls which Nehemiah had built around Jerusalem—which were supposed to separate physically the Jews from the heathen—were the expression of a fundamental inner segregation and religious intolerance. God is God and we are His people—this is the alpha and omega of Jewish belief until the present day. 'The Jew is the teacher of all intolerance, of all fanatical belief, of all that which calls for murder in the name of religion; he appeals to tolerance only when he feels himself threatened, has never practised it and, according to his own laws, cannot practise it.' Chamberlain says this in his *Grundlagen des XIX Jahrhunderts*, whose service to the German people was to be proven only at a later time. These words are totally irreproachable. For example, since the earliest times, it was the Jews who persecuted Christians when they could, and also called upon the heathen to suppress them. When Julian the Apostate again imported the heathen cult, the Jews in Syria seized the opportunity to organize, with redoubled effort, the persecution of Christians. Later, when the Jews had become numerous on Cyprus, they decided to kill all the other inhabitants in one night. This momentous decision cost the lives of

240,000 non-Jews.* Tertullian says that in Carthage at
the time of the persecution of Christians, the Jews took
pleasure in carrying about a painted image, which
showed a man with the ears and feet of an ass holding in
his hand a book with the inscription, THE GOD OF THE
CHRISTIANS.

... Here also it must be emphasized again that the
situation would not be altered if the Jew denied the Talmud, because the national character, which remains the
same, would continue to represent an equally inflexible,
dogmatic viewpoint in other areas. We see this today in
public life, e.g. in the precepts which represent the
socialist conception of the world. I am not going to talk
about the economic measures and proposals of Marxism;
but want only to call attention to the underlying principle
of intolerance which, up to now, has underlaid its entire
being. Communistic thinking had been formed long before
Marx. However, the clever Jew welded it together and
moulded it into a rigid form. Later, we will speak about
the Jewish spirit and about that determination which represents the centre of the Jewish character. Here, as previously
in the Talmud, every variety of rigid, negative credo was
accentuated. With the same doctrinaire infallibility as
in the great synagogue after Ezra, Marx and Lassalle
[sic] swore upon their manifesto. And this rigidity of
dogma had success, like any consistent doctrine which
provides an answer for every question and precludes
debate.

If there comes a time in which men's animation,
flexibility and strength of resistance are weakened, they
flee to those who promise imperturbable security, heaven
or paradise on earth; and, rigid as never before, the Jewish

* Mommsen, *Römische Geschichte*.

spirit, in this case in its atheistic form, stands at the head of those preaching the brutal class struggle. Naturally, whenever it comes to a *fight* the Jewish leaders collectively disappear into the background, unconsciously adhering to the Talmudic principle: 'Draw thyself away from war; do not draw thyself apart from the head of it, but in the end, in order, that thou canst move in again, ally thyself with those who sneer at turmoil. Canaan has taught its sons five things; to love one another, to love theft, to love dissolution, to hate thy master and never to speak the truth.'*

... Morality, for example, subsists in a feeling that rests within us as that 'softly audible voice' which, according to Goethe, 'is what to do, what to shun'. It expresses itself in human society in moral commands and state laws; these are the technical aspects of morality. The more clearly and the more certainly the feeling for justice and injustice is rooted in a people, the less is its need for complicated juridical arrangements; and it will possess that *Kultur* of soul. Therefore it is totally erroneous to see in minute commands and prohibitions in daily life an expression of high consciousness.

On the contrary: it is a sign that the balance of morality does not lie in men, but that it is to be expressed only when praise and punishment for adherence to it is decisive. And here, it is characteristic of the Jewish spirit that a simple morality of good and evil has led to a confusion of laws and to a centuries-long commentary upon them. There are 39 paragraphs on forbidden activities for the Sabbath alone; on Mount Sinai, Moses is supposed to have received 365 prohibitions and 248 commands. Jewish law, however, built thousands of instructions upon this

* Traktat Pesachim, 113a, 113b ff.

foundation, instructions which were to be rigidly observed. Here, it is no longer the question of expression of moral feeling, but merely of knowledge and mastery of technical rules. Jesaya perceived this when he said, 'Because thy people worship me only externally, therefore its wise men shall lose their wisdom, and their men of reason, their reason.'

Those who knew the law were also the most honoured of men; their names are known in all those lands inhabited by Jews in which learning in itself dominates. So great was the reverence for pure knowledge as such, that even a learned Goy was occasionally viewed as a man. Father Samuel forbade men (i.e. Jews) from having relationships with the Goy.* On this, Rabbi Meir said, 'A man must recite three blessings every day: that God has not made me into a Goy, into a woman or into an ignorant one.' Thus, it is even declared possible to have relationships with a learned Goy.

A fundamental difference between varieties of knowledge must be pointed out. For one could easily remark that the Indians also had an accumulated body of knowledge which could be mastered only after decades of work, and that they must have had a spirit related to that of the Jews. With regard to this, we must perceive that the knowledge of the Indian sprang from a longing for the realization of world-coherence (or unity) and amounted to a refined and symbolic perception: that therefore this knowledge served only as means to a goal which transcended it. Throughout his entire history, the Jew has directed his search towards perception in itself, has shunned any metaphysical thinking like the plague. He has instinctively persecuted the few exceptions who flirted with philosophy.

* Bechoroth, 20 ff.

Perception of the law was a goal in itself for the Jew.*

... Zunz calls Judaism the whim of his soul. Now the Jew cannot break loose from this 'whim' even if he is baptized ten times over, and the necessary result of this influence will always be the same: lifelessness, anti-Christianity and materialism.

This is the insight which we obtain from studying the history of the Jewish spirit. Technical works arise from religion and philosophy, and even the greatest of the Jews are no exception. If one takes the trouble to read the *Moreh Nebukim* of Maimonides—a giant of enormous erudition—† one will see that it is devoid of any real spiritual greatness. Many would mention Spinoza. However, according to Jowett it is no longer doubted that Spinoza's entire thought was indebted to the spirits of two men: Descartes and Giordano Bruno. As a true Jewish technician, he succeeded in carrying out the feat of bringing these opposites together under a common denominator, and combining them in a calculated 'system'. That he could do this shows that he understood neither of them. However, the fact that Spinoza flirted with old-Aryan pantheism naturally excited the bitterest opposition of the Jews at that time. However, in the construction of the system, he was as Jewish as only a rabbi could be. He candidly affirmed that everything could be explained in the most convenient manner, without having to have recourse to mystery or secret.

... The Jewish spirit expresses itself in science and art in exactly the same fashion as it did in morals and religion.

* However, where knowledge was not in itself the goal, it was then viewed as a means not to perception, but to power and riches. Among others it is said in Sota 21b ff, 'As soon as wisdom arises in men, so also does cunning.'

† See Munk's translation, *Le guide des égarées* (Paris, 1856).

The Jews pride themselves on having contributed, in all ages, a great number of prominent men in science, particularly in the field of medicine. They say that almost every king had a Jewish physician — upon whom he was able to rely more than on his Christian colleagues.

Moreover, it is indisputable that the natural influence which a physician exerts upon an invalid provided, from the Jewish point of view, a strong incentive for men in this profession and opened a broad field for speculation, one which was utilized in the fullest possible measure. However, we will admit that Jews have had other interests in medicine. We might have expected that they would have had to have been first to establish scientific anatomy. But this is completely wrong. The indomitable drive for discovery which inspired a Leonardo, and which compelled him — under threat of death — to study anatomy in cellars and describe the functions of the muscles in sketches of such phenomenal exactness that they have not been improved upon till this day ... none of this has found a counterpart in Jewish scientists. With all their knowledge, they lack intuition of genius and creative strength. Since Kant, we have differentiated precisely between understanding [*Verstand*] and reason [*Vernunft*]. With the former term we associate the ability to gather together sensuously-mediated data to form a picture and then tie it together under forms of causality. With the latter term we mean the ability to bind together all judgments of understanding into a unity. Understanding creates knowledge; reason creates science-formal knowledge. If, on the other hand, reason comprehends the given, it is nevertheless spontaneously active, and in the capacity of a bold, direction-giving idea, it pushes the feeler towards new discoveries. The idea of the atom, the law of the conservation of energy, the ether theory [*sic*]—these are not things which any fool could formalize; they cannot be proven logically and empirically without further ado. They are forward-reaching attempts of creative reason, 'precise, sensuous phantasy', as Goethe called it, which goes hand in hand with irreproachable empirical investigation.

It is now not difficult to delineate with great clarity the sphere of the Jewish spirit. From time immemorial it has mastered that region of science which has been occupied with understanding. That lack of phantasy and inner searching, damned to fruitlessness by the religion and philosophy of the Jews, is reflected in science as well. Not one single creative scientific idea has sprung from the brain of a Jew; he has never been a pathfinder.

*   *   *

Rosenberg condemns the Jews for uncreativity, something that was reflected in their materialism. This, says Rosenberg, was the curse of the nineteenth century.

... Do not misunderstand me. I am not at all maintaining that the Jew bears sole guilt for the bestial materialization of our life; but I am holding strongly to the fact that he placed his entire power, in terms of energy and money, at the disposal of a tendency which was all-alienating, and that he had to do this to remain in harmony with his centuries-old essence. Left to itself, the German character would have achieved a balance. However, this was made impossible due to Jewish strength in the press, theatre, trade and sciences. We ourselves have been guilty—we should not have emancipated the Jews but, as Goethe, Fichte and Herder vainly demanded, should have created insurmountable exceptional laws for them. One does not allow a poison to drift about un- observed, nor grant it parity with medicine; rather one keeps it within careful limits. After 2,000 years, this has finally happened in the National Socialist Reich!

*   *   *

Naturally, Rosenberg claimed that the Jewish soul, materialistic and unspiritual, was also reflected in Jewish aesthetics.

... The Jewish art dealer of today asks only for those works which could excite sensuality, and the same is done by Jewish theatre-directors, publishers, etc. Today, our Jewish critics do not conduct their investigations according to serious form-will, but according to technique, i.e. the manufacture of a work. Thus, Jewish artists have clear sailing; for if the standard is an external one, they can easily recognize it themselves. Three hundred years ago, the much-praised Max Liebermann could never have received the recognition which he enjoys today. This man has his place in art history as the peddler of French art and, because of this, his importance has also been exhausted. The techniques of his paintings could be highly striking, but they could not disguise their inner emptiness. The older and more superficial Liebermann became, the more effects filled his paintings. The young Jews are, for the most part, ensconced in the camp of artistic Bolshevism and Futurism. Until 1933, it was one of the insanities of our time that the representatives of this crudeness knew the most about the soul and inexpres- sible inner experience.

A typical example of the Jewish art-spirit is to be found

in the virtuosos who blanketed Europe. With the greatest
bravado, singers, violinists and pianists master their
instruments; actors play their roles with great pomposity;
and Jewish theatre-directors master stage techniques with
a refinement which can hardly be excelled. But, again, all
these Jewish prodigies, all these virtuosos, have they
become creative artists? They have attempted to force
quality through quantity and to produce art through
sensual means. Mahler had in mind, as an ideal, the
one-thousand-voiced orchestra, while Reinhardt began a
theatre circus with hundreds and hundreds of players.
Everything in order to overwhelm the public ...

V. THE IDEAL STATE

A few articles will suffice to show the image of Utopia which Rosenberg identified with the Nazi state. 'Totaler Staat?', Völkischer Beobachter, January 9th, 1934, in Gestaltung der Idee, Blut und Ehre II. Band, Reden und Aufsätze von 1933–1935 herausgegeben von Thilo von Trotha (München, 1936).

The revolution of January 30th, 1933, was in no way the continuation of the old absolutist state, even under a new emblem. Rather, the state assumed a different relationship with regard to the *Volk* and *Volkstum* from what it had in 1918; but also one which was different from the one of 1871. What has been completed during this past year, and what remains to be completed over a broader radius, is not the so-called totality of the state, but the totality of the National Socialist movement. The state is no longer an entity which, be it close to the party and the movement or be it a mechanical apparatus, is a ruling instrument; rather it is an instrument of the National Socialist *Weltanschauung*. On the surface, this would appear to be merely a trifling difference in emphasis between state-political and perception-critical forms of thought. And yet, clarification of the intellectual presuppositions is of great importance, because a false conceptual picture will yield—if not right away, then most certainly in the course of time—practical consequences for political action. If we continue to speak of the total state, younger National Socialists and coming generations will gradually shift the state concept into the centre of things, and the activities of state officials will be felt to be the primary ones. If, however, we emphasize with all clarity today that it is a certain political ideology and movement that demands the right of totality, the gaze of generations will be directed upon the movement, and the relationship between state and N.S.D.A.P. will be seen in a totally different light than if one were to designate statishness itself as primary. The National Socialist movement is the moulded strength of twentieth-century thought; moulded for the security of the collective German *Volk* and of its blood and character. The state, as a most powerful and virile instrument, is placed at the disposal of the movement, and its life-strengths and powers are continuously renewed by the movement in order that it remain flexible and capable of resistance while avoiding the dangers of bureaucratization, petrification and estrangement from *Volk*. Only in this connection does the National Socialist state-concept become truly alive, and we even believe that the state itself will gain sanctification through it, and that it will derive inner strength and authority to a greater degree than if it transformed itself into its own goal—even if it were led by energetic individuals, the state would become ossified through this process.

For all these reasons, it behooves National Socialists not to speak any more of the total state, but of the *completion of the National Socialist* Weltanschauung, *of the N.S.D.A.P. as the embodiment of this* Weltanschauung, *and of the National Socialist state as the means by which National Socialism, the mightiest phenomenon originating in the twentieth century, secures soul, intellect and blood.*

*   *   *

In a Königsburg speech, of April 27th, 1934, entitled 'Der deutsche Ordensstaat', we can see the medievally-oriented Romanticism of Rosenberg. In this address, he links the supra-class ideology of the National Socialist part to a supra-political tradition which he sees manifested in the German Orders of the Middle Ages. The devotion of the medieval German to the leader, e.g. Hermann Salza, is carried forth in the devotion of the German people to Führer and Vaterland. *(These extracts, too, are taken from* Gestaltung der Idee*).*

... *The state concept of German man did not lead to an impersonal hierarchical officialdom, nor to a caesar who felt himself to be God and who hovered in unapproachable remoteness; rather, the most important life standard was the personal relationship between liege lord and vassal* ... The relationship, felt as personal, between the German soldier and *General Marshal von Hindenburg*, was one of the secrets of the great success of the German army. In this also there lies the hidden reason why Germany did *not* collapse after the treason of November 8th, 1918, because the figure of Hindenburg, which is a mythical one even today, with all its powers of spiritual tension—*powers which are perhaps unconscious*—carried over into another time; *a time when they could be discharged through a newer, younger nobleman, whom today we call our Führer.*

From its inception, the National Socialist movement has declared that it is not interested in quarrelling over monarchical and republican theories. It was ever conscious that there have been good and bad monarchs in the histories of peoples, as well as strongly moulded and degenerate republics. We know that Ancient Rome, from whose peasant stock later ages drew strength of stature, was a *republic*. All those powers of character which were later shamefully squandered by the Caesars were formed during this time. It is just as plain that *Ancient* Greece was led by kings, and that the form of monarchy had constituted the culture-building fountain-head of Hellas.

German man conducts his life organically, from conceptions of duke to those of monarchy and, for me, it is no accident that while almost every people has slain princes in bloody revolutions, German history tells of no case in which a German has beheaded a king.

A purely republican government in Germany would be possible only if the people had a common temperament and self-discipline, perhaps in a few districts. However this could hardly be, *in view of the variety of characteristics embraced by a people of seventy million.*

*   *   *

Rosenberg claims that the Danube region and the countries of the Baltic area (Östseeraum) must be bound together and that all of them — presumably not just Germany — should prosper.

Contemporary Germany feels itself to be inwardly strong enough to say this openly, without allowing itself to be governed by so-called considerations of prestige: we have renounced that old, petty cabinet diplomacy in the conviction that some day all peoples will consider and solve this Eastern question without any form of narrow-mindedness. *We believe that the great community of destiny, Scandinavia and the Baltic peoples, stands above and beyond different systems of government and internal political principles.* Therefore, we welcome it if, here in Lübeck, representatives of *spiritual* Scandinavia stand next to political and economic representatives. Through this we know that it has shown itself to be truly worthy of its great mission; and we perceive in the attitude of one of the greatest Norwegian poets, Knut Hamsun, towards the new Germany a guarantee that all other fighters for European community understand with him the great struggle of the German people; that they are gaining an awareness of the goal of the collective spiritual consciousness of Nordic and Baltic lands — not in the sense of its being a doctrine which has to be forced upon all other peoples from above, but as an unbiased judgment of all life-necessities pressing up from below.

If, for the most part, the Nordic Society which has assembled today already desires to nurture a cultural and economic community among the Northern states and Baltic peoples, there is linked with this the hope that, above and beyond all division, similar serious efforts will become even stronger in the destiny-area of the Baltic so that, in this region also, true spiritual, economic and political satisfaction will press onward as further evidence of the many-sided European consciousness.

We are happy to hold this first great Nordic day here in *Lübeck*. At one time, Lübeck had a fateful influence upon the Baltic which, for us, is so much like home. And even if times and forms have changed, even if German ships no longer have to journey through the Baltic as did the warrior Koggens, we nevertheless rejoice that, faithful to its old traditions, the head of the former Hansa once again promises to be a centre of a new variety of co-operation of Nordic and Baltic peoples — not through one-sided emphasis upon Lübeck's interests, but animated by the high consciousness of fulfilling a great duty; the duty of inwardly grasping the laws of destiny of our time, and leading all who pass by into a collective effort.

So today we greet the old, noble Hansa city. We also greet all the officers of the Nordic Society in Germany. We extend our greetings over the sea to all those people in other states who, in like fashion, are honestly compelled to get to grips with the tasks of *our* time, to work on them and to work in common for the well-being of our old Europe—to work for the best for *each* Northern and Baltic people, and for the linking of the European destiny with the well-being of every single nation.

Europe is not to be conceived of as a lifeless debating society, but as a region of territories marked out by destiny. Deeply rooted in its individual lines of will, the region can produce a unity only through impartial delimitation; a unity which, firmly rooted and experienced, will one day be strong enough collectively to protect a thousand-year-old *Kultur*, a thousand-year-old humanity, and to secure for it necessities of life from all remaining continents and peoples of the earth.

BIBLIOGRAPHY

The dates given are those of the years of first publication.

The works of Alfred Rosenberg

An die Dunkelmänner unserer Zeit (München, 1935). This is an answer to Catholic attacks on Rosenberg's *Mythus*.

Blut und Ehre, ein Kampf für deutsche Wiedergeburt, Reden und Aufsätze von 1919–1933, herausgegeben von Thilo von Trotha (München, 1935). Collection of Rosenberg's speeches and articles between 1919 and 1933.

Der deutsche Ordensstaat (München, 1934). An offprint of his April 27th, 1934 speech of this name.

Die Entwicklung der deutschen Freiheitsbewegung (München, 1933). Obviously, an attempt to identify National Socialism with German freedom.

Europa und sein Todfeind; vier Reden über das bolshewistische Problem (München, 1938). An offprint of four of Rosenberg's speeches against Bolshevism.

Der Fall Ludendorff (München, n.d.). A glorification of Ludendorff, who marched with Hitler in the ill-fated *putsch* attempt of November 1923.

Freimauerische Weltpolitik im lichte der kritischen Forschung (München, 1931). An elaboration upon Rosenberg's theories regarding Freemason/Jewish world conspiracies.

Friedrich Nietzsche. Zentralverlag der N.S.D.A.P., Franz Eher Nachf. (München). An offprint of his speech of October 14th, 1944.

Der geschichtliche Sinn unseres Kampfes; Rede von Reichsleiter Rosenberg vor Soldaten der Westfront, 16. April, 1940 (Berlin, 1940).

Gestaltung der Idee, Blut und Ehre II. Band, Reden und Aufsätze von 1933–1935, herausgegeben von Thilo von Trotha (München, 1936). Collection of Rosenberg's speeches and articles between 1933 and 1935.

Houston Stewart Chamberlain als Verkünder und Begründer einer deutschen Zukunft (München, 1927). A tribute to Houston

Stewart Chamberlain, one of the four 'sources', Rosenberg says, of National Socialism (the others were Wagner, Lagarde and Nietzsche). Much of this appears, in shortened form, in *Mythus*.

Die internationale Hochfinanz (München, n.d.). A concentrated attack on Jewish control of the world economy. An elaboration upon themes found in *Die Spur des Juden im Wandel der Zeiten* (1920).

Judentum, Jesuitismus, Deutsches Christentum (München, 1932). Rosenberg contrasts the perfidious Judaic tradition and that of the Jesuits with true Germanic Christianity.

Kampf um die Macht, Blut und Ehre III. Band, Aufsätze von 1921–1932, herausgegeben von Thilo von Trotha (München, 1938). A collection of Rosenberg's essays written between 1921 and 1932. Most of these essays first appeared in *Völkischer Beobachter*.

Krisis und neubau Europas (Berlin, 1934). An attempt to link Germany's rebirth as a Nordic power to the salvation of Europe.

Letzte Aufzeichnungen; Ideale und Idole der nationalsozialistischen Revolution (Göttingen, 1954), translated from the German by Eric Posselt as *Memoirs of Alfred Rosenberg*, with commentary by Serge Lang and Ernst von Schenck (Chicago, 1949). Rosenberg's memoirs, written while in prison awaiting execution as a war criminal. In comparison to Rosenberg's earlier works this one is, understandably, somewhat subdued.

Der Mythus des 20. Jahrhunderts (München, 1930). Rosenberg's major work. Here, all of his basic ideas on race, *Volk*, religion and state were constructed into something of a philosophical system.

Neugeburt Europas als werdende Geschichte (Halle, Saale, 1934). Rosenberg identifies Europe's rebirth with that of the Nordic race as embodied in Germany.

Novemberköpfe (München, 1939). A critique of the Social Democrats and their respective roles in the formation of the Weimar Republic.

Pest in Russland (München, 1922). An analysis of the role of Jews and the Jewish conspiracy in the Bolshevik Revolution.

Politisches Tagebuch aus den Jahren 1934/1935 und 1939/1940, edited by H. G. Seraphim (1956). A diary set down during these years.

Protestantische Rompilger (München, 1934?). An answer to Protestant critics of *Mythus*.

Die Religion Meister Eckhart (München, 1934). Taken from Rosenberg's *Mythus*.

Die Spur des Juden im Wandel der Zeiten (München, 1920). Rosenberg's most comprehensive and detailed attack on Judaism.

Der Staatsfeindliche Zionismus (München, 1921). A critique of the Jewish world-conspiracy as embodied in Zionism.

Der Sumpf (München, n.d.). Here, Rosenberg compares the Weimar Republic to a 'swamp', emphasizing its 'degeneracy' and 'corruption'.

Die Totengräber Russlands (München, 1921). In this work, Rosenberg attacks the Bolshevik Jews as being the 'gravediggers' of Russia.

Unmoral im Talmud (München, 1920). Offprint of essay of this title. An attack upon the anti-Christian aspects of the Talmud.

Verbrechen der Freimauerei (München, 1927). An attack upon the conspiratorial crimes of Freemasonry.

Der Weltverschwörer kongress zu Basel (München, 1927). Here, Rosenberg focuses upon the Zionist Congress at Basel and their 'adherence' to the horrible *Protocols of the Elders of Zion*.

Wesen, Grundsätze und Ziele der N.S.D.A.P. (München, 1923). This is an elaboration upon the original 25 points put down by Anton Drexler in 1920, before the German Workers' Party became the National Socialist German Workers' Party. After 1933, it became the official Nazi programme.

Das Wesensgefüge des Nationalsozialismus (München, 1932). Calls for a 'German rebirth' through support of the National Socialist Party.

Der Zukunftsweg einer deutschen Aussenpolitik (München, 1927). Here, expansionism is justified on the basis of Nordic history destiny and *Lebensraum*.

Books edited by Alfred Rosenberg

Dietrich Eckart, ein Vermächtnis. Selected works of Dietrich Eckart, edited and introduced by Alfred Rosenberg (München, 1928). Dietrich Eckart was a somewhat Bohemian poet, virulently anti-Semitic, who was until his death in 1923, a great influence upon both Hitler and Rosenberg.

Gougenot des Mousseaux, *Le Juif* was translated by Rosenberg as, *Der Jude, das Judentum, und die Verjudung der christlichen Völker* (München, 1921). Gougenot des Mousseaux was a notorious French racist of the nineteenth century, second in importance only to Count Arthur de Gobineau.

Die Protokollen der Weisen von Zion, edited and introduced by Alfred Rosenberg. (München, 1923.) *The Protocols of the Elders of Zion,* perhaps the most famous anti-Semitic doctrine of modern times, appeared in Russia during the first decade of the 20th century. It was a cheap forgery which was supposed to be a Jewish plan for the take-over of the world. Alfred Rosenberg helped to spread its fame in Germany, while Henry Ford performed the same service in the United States.

A selected bibliography of writings on or about Alfred Rosenberg

Up to now, there has been no work devoted solely to Rosenberg. However, there are a number of books and articles in which he is discussed along with various aspects of his writings and policies.

Billig, J. (Ed.), *Centre de documentation juive contemporaine.* Alfred Rosenberg dans l'action idéologique, politique et administrative du Reich Hitlérien inventaire commonté de la collection de documents conservés au C.D.J.C. provenant des archives du Reichsleiter et ministre A. Rosenberg (Paris, 1963).

Brenner, Hildegard, *Die Kunstpolitik des Nationalsozialismus* (Hamburg, 1963). The most thorough-going study of Nazi art policy to date. Contains much interesting material on the respective views of Goebbels, Rosenberg and Hitler on art.

Bullock, Alan, *Hitler, A Study in Tyranny* (London, 1952; New York, 1960). This work contains some very interesting material on Rosenberg's early influence upon Hitler, and on his position and relationships within the Nazi Party.

Clark, Alan, *Barbarossa, The Russian-German Conflict 1941–1945* (London, 1965; New York, 1965). Although this is primarily a military history, this work does contain some valuable information on the political activities of Rosenberg while *Reichsminister* for the Eastern territories. His conflicts with Erich Koch, Reichskommissar for the Ukraine, are well documented in this work. Rosenberg hoped to use a native Ukrainian resistance movement against the Soviet Union, while Koch, more representative of the wishes of Hitler and Himmler, opted for slavery and/or extermination.

Dallin, Alexander, *German Rule in Russia, 1941–1945* (London, 1957). The most comprehensive study of German civil and military authority in the occupied areas of the Soviet Union. Rosenberg's role as Reichsminister is frequently discussed, as are the conflicts between him and various civilian and SS leaders.

Davidson, Eugene, *The Trial of the Germans: Nuremberg 1945-1946* (New York, 1966). In this work, the most detailed study of the Nuremberg trials available in English, Davidson, like many others, tends to view Rosenberg as a somewhat muddled idealist. Of particular interest are Davidson's descriptions of Rosenberg's clashes with other Nazi big-wigs over occupation policy in Russia.

Fest, Joachim C., *The Face of the Third Reich* (first published in Munich in 1963 as *Gesicht des dritten Reiches;* translated from the German by Michael Bullock, Brattleboro, Vermont, 1970.) In this work, which consists of cameo portraits of all the Nazi leaders, Fest treats Rosenberg as a sort of tragic figure who really believed in those National Socialist principles which were being rapidly abandoned by the more realistic practitioners of power. Fest's portrayal of Rosenberg as a sort of pathetic idealist tends to obscure the real brutality that was to be found even in such esoteric works as *Der Mythus des 20. Jahrhunderts.*

Gilbert, G. M., *Nuremberg Diary* (London, 1948; New York, 1947). G. M. Gilbert was prison psychologist at the Nuremberg trial of the Nazi war criminals. His book contains some fascinating insights into the personality of Rosenberg, among others. Among other things, we learn of his unwillingness to take any responsibility for the consequences of his ideological pronouncements and that all but seven of the Nazi leaders on trial ranked higher than Rosenberg on the Wechsler-Bellvue intelligence test (Rosenberg obtained a score of 127).

————, *The Psychology of Dictatorship* (New York, 1950). This work is essentially an elaboration upon the conclusions and results described by Gilbert in *Nuremberg Diary*.

Goebbels, Josef, *The Goebbels Diaries, 1942–1943*, edited, translated and introduced by Louis P. Lochner (London, 1949; New York, 1948). Here, we get a most unflattering view of Rosenberg, whom Goebbels treats as a fuzzy-minded, impractical and occasionally trecherous incompetent.

Jackson, Robert H., *The Nürnberg Case* (New York, 1947). An interesting description of the proceedings at Nuremberg, written by the United States Chief Counsel for the Prosecution.

Kelley, Douglas, *Twenty-Two Cells at Nuremberg* (London, 1947; New York, 1947). A somewhat more formal but less detailed study than that of Gilbert's of the attitudes and reactions of the Nazi leaders on trial. Kelley was prison psychiatrist at Nuremberg during the months of October and November 1945.

Laqueur, Walter, *Russia and Germany, A Century of Conflict* (London, 1965; Boston, 1965). A fascinating study of the influences, mostly negative it would seem, that Russia and Germany had upon one another between the mid-1880s and the Second World War. Laqueur assiduously documents the influence of Russian reactionary and racist thinking upon Rosenberg during the post-revolutionary period.

Mosse, George L., *The Crisis of German Ideology* (London, 1966; New York, 1964). The most comprehensive study extant

of the history of *Volkish* ideology and the organizations that espoused it. Contains information on Rosenberg's contacts and ideological confrères after the First World War.
——(Ed.), *Nazi Culture* (London, 1966; New York, 1966). This book contains a fascinating collection of documents from the Nazi period. Among them are several selections written by Rosenberg. One of these is taken from *Mythus* and concerns female emancipation. Here, we get a view of the petit-bourgeois side of Rosenberg who, in the finest Victorian tradition, maintains that the woman's place is in the home, to which nature has assigned her. The other essay is taken from his edited work on Dietrich Eckart and concerns the 'wordly nature' of the Jew.

Neumann, Franz, *Behemoth, The Structure and Practice of National Socialism 1933–1944* (London, 1942; 2nd revised edition, New York, 1944). This massive study of the Nazi Party and its organization contains some interesting material on Rosenberg, particularly with regard to his attitude towards the state. Neumann goes into some detail in describing the clash between Rosenberg's view of the state, which saw it as subordinate to *Volk* and to the party which embodies the will of the *Volk*, and that of Carl Schmitt, a Nazi political theoretician who placed the state in a more prominent position.

Schoenbaum, David, *Hitler's Social Revolution: Class and Status in Nazi Germany 1933–1939* (New York, 1966). This book is a negative study of Rosenberg, among others, in as much as it describes how much of the woolly mysticism in which Nazism was ensconced was eventually sacrificed to the demands of day-to-day economic and social realities.

Shirer, William L., *The Rise and Fall of the Third Reich* (London, 1960; New York, 1960). While Shirer's description of the intellectual background of Nazism is somewhat weak, his study of the party structure itself, and Rosenberg's role within it, is valuable.

Viereck, Peter, *Metapolitics: The Roots of the Nazi Mind* (New York, 1961). Revised edition of *Metapolitics: From the Romantics to Hitler* (New York, 1941). The most detailed study of Rosenberg's *Mythus* available. In the 1961 work,

Viereck has added an essay concerning the influence of Rosenberg's ideology and his policies in Russia.

Wulf, Josef (Ed.), *Bildungskunst im dritten Reich* (Gütersloh, 1964). One of four books, edited by Wulf, on culture in Nazi Germany. This volume contains much interesting data on *Volk*-aesthetics.

Naturally, much material can be found in *The Trial of the Major War Criminals Before the International Military Tribunal.* See *Proceedings,* vols. 1–23 and *Documents in Evidence,* vols. 24–42.

Articles

Alexander Bein, 'Der jüdische Parasit; Bemerkungen zur Semantik der Judenfrage', *Vierteljahrshefte für Zeitgeschichte,* 13 Jhrg., 2. Heft (April 1965). An interesting and valuable study of the history of the 'Jewish parasite' concept, with particular emphasis upon the use made of this term by Alfred Rosenberg.

Hildegard Brenner, 'Die Kunst im politischen Machtkampf 1933/1934', *Vierteljahrshefte für Zeitgeschichte,* 10 Jhrg., 2. Heft (January 1962). This article describes the clash over art policy that developed within the Nazi Party during the years mentioned. Of particular interest is the quarrelling that took place between Rosenberg and Goebbels, whose respective views on art differed greatly, at least then.

J. P. Fox, 'Alfred Rosenberg in London', *Contemporary Review,* 213 (July 1968). This describes Rosenberg's visit to London in 1933 and his failure to win either friends or royal support for the Nazi government.

Robert A. Pois, 'German Expressionism in the Plastic Art and the Nazis: A Confrontation of Idealists', *German Life and Letters,* vol. XXI, no. 3 (April 1968). A study of the similarities and differences between the Nazi view of art, as represented by Rosenberg, and that of the German Expressionists. Rosenberg's aesthetic is discussed in some detail.

71 72 73 10 9 8 7 6 5 4 3 2 1